Fairground PHYSICS

Motion, Momentum, and Magnets
with Hands-On Science Activities

Angie Smibert
Illustrated by Micah Rauch

Titles in the **Build It Yourself Accessible Science** Set

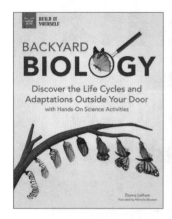 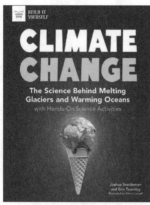  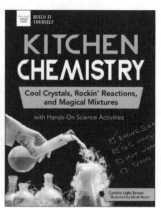

Check out more titles at www.nomadpress.net

Nomad Press

A division of Nomad Communications

10 9 8 7 6 5 4 3 2 1

This book was manufactured by Versa Press, East Peoria, Illinois
March 2020, Job #J19-12319
ISBN Softcover: 978-1-61930-891-6
ISBN Hardcover: 978-1-61930-888-6

Educational Consultant, Marla Conn

Questions regarding the ordering of this book should be addressed to
Nomad Press
2456 Christian St., White River Junction, VT 05001
www.nomadpress.net

Printed in the United States.

CONTENTS

Interested in Primary Sources? Look for this icon.

Use a smartphone or tablet app to scan the QR code and explore more! Photos are also primary sources because a photograph takes a picture at the moment something happens. You can find a list of URLs on the Resources page. If the QR code doesn't work, try searching the internet with the Keyword Prompts to find other helpful sources.

🔎 fairground physics

HEAT

WAVES

FORCES

ENERGY

MOTION

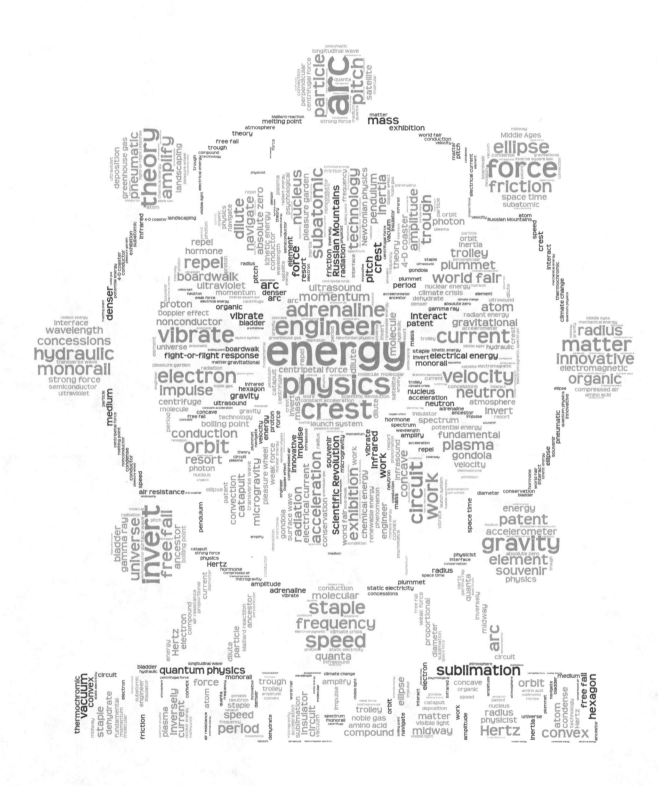

WELCOME TO
THE FAIR!

Every year, millions of people flock to fairgrounds and amusement parks seeking thrills, adventure, and maybe even some tasty food. And every year, engineers try to make taller, faster, and twistier rides—all in the name of fun!

Imagine you're strapped into a new ride—the Maxx Force. **Compressed air** launches the roller coaster forward, slamming you back into the padded restraints. In two seconds, you rocket up the first loop at 78 miles per hour. For a moment, you feel weightless—and then your stomach drops. The cars (and riders!) flip around—twice—at a gut-wrenching 60 miles per hour.

ESSENTIAL QUESTION

What makes fairgrounds fun?

WORDS TO KNOW

engineer: someone who uses science, math, and creativity to design and build things.

compressed air: air under more pressure than the outside air.

1

The **FASTEST** roller coaster is the **FORMULA ROSSA** at Ferrari World in the United Arab Emirates. The coaster can reach speeds of **149 MILES PER HOUR.**

Before it glides home, the roller coaster **inverts** three more times—and breaks as many records. The newest roller coaster at Six Flags Great America in Gurnee, Illinois, set the records for fastest launch, tallest double inversion, and fastest inversion. Coaster fans are lining up to try the Maxx Force!

What makes a ride such as this fun—and even a little bit scary? **Physics**! In one roller coaster ride, you've taken a master class in physics. You've experienced the **force** of **gravity**. You even felt **microgravity** in **free fall**, much as astronauts do! You've created and expended **energy**. You've moved in straight lines, loops, and twists.

In fact, all the rides at the fairground or amusement park depend on physics. So do the foods, lights, music, and games! To design rides, engineers have to understand motion, forces, and energy in order to make the rides safe and fun.

Want to see what it's like to ride Maxx Force? **This animation puts you in the front seat of the coaster!**

🔍 Coasterforce Maxx Force

PS

WHAT IS PHYSICS?

Physics is the study of how the **universe** works. We humans have been pondering this for thousands of years. Ancient Greek philosophers tried to explain what makes up **matter**, as well as how it moves. They observed the world around them and offered reasoned explanations. One early philosopher even correctly described matter as being made up of **atoms**.

The tallest roller coaster is the KINGDA KA at Six Flags New Jersey. The coaster is 456 FEET TALL.

However, a more famous thinker, named Aristotle (384–322 **BCE**) rejected this idea. He didn't think a **vacuum**—such as the empty spaces between the atoms—could exist. He proposed that objects needed a force behind them to move—and keep moving. For example, if someone threw a ball, it kept moving, Aristotle reasoned, because air rushed in behind the ball to keep a vacuum from forming. His inaccurate ideas about motion ruled physics until the sixteenth century.

Does this ride look fun to you?

WORDS TO KNOW

theory: an unproven idea that explains why something is the way it is.

physicist: a scientist who studies physics.

Scientific Revolution: a series of events and discoveries between the 1500s and 1700s that marked the emergence of modern science.

Newtonian physics: the science that uses the laws of motion and gravitation formulated in the late seventeenth century by English physicist Sir Isaac Newton to explain how matter behaves.

electromagnetism: magnetism created by a current of electricity.

radiation: energy that comes from a source and travels through something, such as the radiation from an X-ray that travels through a person.

subatomic: relating to the inside of an atom.

That's when Galileo Galilei (1564–1642) did something radical. He performed experiments to test his ideas about motion. In his most famous experiment, Galileo claimed to have dropped two objects—one heavy, one light—from the top of the Leaning Tower of Pisa in 1589. Both objects reached the ground at the same time.

ALL OBJECTS on Earth FALL at the same rate.

Although some scholars do not believe that Galileo actually performed this experiment, Galileo argued—correctly!—that objects free fall at the same rate, no matter their size. Through other experiments, Galileo also concluded that an object in motion continues to move in a straight line until it's stopped by some force. Both **theories** are still accepted today!

Throughout the next few hundred years, other **physicists** built on Galileo's ideas—and used experiments to prove them. This period is known as the **Scientific Revolution**.

Can you see why this would be a good place to test Galileo's theory of free fall?

Watch *Apollo* astronaut David Scott repeat Galileo's experiment on the moon.

🔍 hammer feather moon

Now, watch physicist Brian Cox repeat the same experiment in a vacuum chamber at NASA's Space Power Facility in Cleveland, Ohio. Can you reproduce the experiment? Why do scientists continue to repeat experiments after a concept has been proved or disproved?

🔍 Brian Cox BBC vacuum

Sir Isaac Newton (1642–1727) improved on Galileo's laws of motion and discovered gravity. (We'll discuss the laws of motion in more detail when we explore the bumper cars!)

According to Newton's laws of gravity, every mass in the universe is attracted to every other mass. That attraction is called gravity. Its pull depends on the size of the objects and the distance between them. Newton's laws of both motion and gravity formed the basis of what's often called classical or **Newtonian physics**. We still study this today.

Since Newton, other physicists have made discoveries about **electromagnetism**, light, heat, **radiation**, and other forces. By the late nineteenth and early twentieth centuries, physicists focused more and more on matter and energy at a very small scale—the **subatomic** level.

FAIRGROUND PHYSICS

All matter is made up of atoms, and atoms are composed of even smaller particles. Physicists discovered that matter and energy behave in strange, even whacky ways at the particle level. They found that energy, for instance, isn't a smooth spectrum or flow. Energy comes in packets called **quanta**. These new discoveries, which came at the beginning of the twentieth century, led to a new branch of physics called **quantum physics**.

Even in the quirky world of quantum physics, though, physics boils down to the study of matter and energy. In fact, that's what physicists think the universe is made of. Matter is anything that has mass and takes up space. It can be the smallest particle in an atom, a galaxy, or anything in between. Energy can exist in many forms. Energy is the ability to do work, such as move a roller coaster up a hill or split an atom. Physicists study how matter and energy work together.

Any matter that is in motion has energy, which brings us back to fairgrounds and amusement parks. Everything is in some kind of motion, from the spinning Ferris wheel to the frying funnel cake. That's why it's the perfect place to study physics!

Who wants a funnel cake?

Many physics teachers take their classes to amusement parks! Why? Not just because it's fun—fairgrounds and amusement parks are excellent places to study physics. We'll take a look at bumper cars, pendulum rides, dunk tanks, fairground food, and more to discover how the laws of physics make it possible to experience all of these things. So, strap on your safety harness and let's go!

Good Science Practices

Every good scientist keeps a science journal! Scientists use the scientific method to keep their experiments organized. Choose a notebook to use as your science journal. As you read through this book and do the activities, keep track of your observations and record each step in a scientific method worksheet, like the one shown here.

Question: What are we trying to find out? What problem are we trying to solve?

Research: What is already known about the problem?

Hypothesis/Prediction: What do we think the answer will be?

Equipment: What supplies are we using?

Method: What procedure are we following?

Results: What happened? Why?

Each chapter of this book begins with an essential question to help guide your exploration of physics. Keep the question in your mind as you read the chapter. At the end of each chapter, use your science journal to record your thoughts and answers.

ESSENTIAL QUESTION

What makes fairgrounds fun?

PHYSICS KIT

° empty plastic water bottle

FREE-FALLING
WATER TRICK

When Galileo dropped objects off the Leaning Tower of Pisa, he was experimenting with free fall. A free-falling object is being pulled toward Earth by gravity. Other forces may be slowing it down. Galileo found that all objects free fall at the same rate, regardless of their mass.

Free fall is also the inspiration for drop tower rides! Riders are strapped into their seats, pulled to the top of a tower—and then released. Brakes prevent the riders from hitting the bottom, of course, but they experience the stomach-dropping thrill of free fall for several seconds. In this project, you'll be experimenting with free-falling water bottles, so you might want to do it outside!

❭ Poke two holes about halfway up the sides of a plastic water bottle. Cover the holes with your fingers and fill the bottle with water.

❭ Hold the bottle upright and still. Uncover the holes. What happens? **Tip:** If the water doesn't flow out, make the holes bigger and refill the bottle.

❭ Cover the holes again and refill the bottle. Hold the bottle at arm's length and drop it straight down. Watch to see if any water pours out while it's falling. What happens? Record your observations and draw the outcome in your science journal.

WHAT'S HAPPENING?

While the bottle is at rest, gravity pulls the water down. The bottle pushes against the water, keeping it in—except where there are holes. In free fall, though, the bottle and water are being pulled down by gravity at the same rate. The water stays in the bottle until it hits the ground.

By the way, when you're experiencing free fall in a drop tower ride, it feels as though you're weightless as you plunge toward the earth. You're not really. You and the seats/restraints are falling at the same rate, so you don't feel them pushing against you—much like the water in the falling water bottle.

Try This!

Drop the bottle at different heights. Time the drops and record the results. How long does it take to drop from different heights? Does the bottle get faster as it approaches the ground? Jot down your observations in your notebook.

DESIGN A SIMPLE
ROLLER COASTER

PHYSICS KIT
° about 6 feet of
  ½-inch foam tubing
° plastic cups, blocks,
  or books for support
° masking tape
° marble

Roller coasters don't have engines to power them around the track. Instead, roller coasters convert **potential energy** into **kinetic energy.** That is, they get energy from their start. Many coasters are pulled up the first slope. While sitting at the top of that hill, the coaster has a lot of potential energy. The coaster will have more energy if the hill is higher or the slope is steeper. Once the cars begin sliding down the slope, that potential energy becomes kinetic energy. That energy powers the coaster up the next hill or loop.

In this experiment, you'll be exploring how high a starting hill needs to be to give your coaster enough energy to make it over a hill or through a loop.

❱ **Cut the foam tubing in half, lengthwise.** You may join the two halves—end to end—with masking tape if you want a really long roller coaster!

❱ **Lay the tubing open-side up on the ground** or table in the shape you'd like your roller coaster to be. This is your roller coaster track.

❱ **Place plastic cups or other supports under the track to create hills.** The first slope should be the tallest! Use the masking tape to attach the track to the cups. You may also need to tape down the track in other places.

❱ **Put the marble on the top of the first hill**—and let it roll! This is your coaster.

❱ **How far does the marble go?** Does it make it up the second hill? Raise the height of the first hill and repeat your experiment! How high does the first hill need to be so the marble makes it around your track? Keep experimenting with the layout of your roller coaster!

Try This!

Add a loop to your track! How high does that first hill need to be now? If you want to make a larger coaster, you can use pool noodles and golf balls!

WORDS TO KNOW

potential energy: energy that is stored.

kinetic energy: energy caused by movement.

Chapter 1

A LITTLE
HISTORY

Humans have gathered for festivals, sporting events, plays, and other amusements since long before they began recording history. What is it like when you and your friends get together for a party or to hang out after school? People have always found fun, excitement, and community from gathering together.

Where did amusement parks and their rides come from? Their history isn't entirely clear. Amusement parks have their roots in European **pleasure gardens**, **world fairs**, **resorts**, **boardwalks**, and other gathering spaces. In fact, the earliest carousel ride dates back to 500 CE. Today, some fairgrounds and amusement parks feature rides that are astounding in their ability to transform the laws of physics into a new flavor of fun. Let's take a look at the roots of these exciting places!

ESSENTIAL QUESTION

Do people love carnival rides today for the same reasons they loved them in the last century?

EUROPEAN PLEASURE GARDENS

Amusement parks, carnivals, and fairs have their beginnings in the European pleasure gardens of the 1500s. Pleasure gardens grew out of parks and other public spaces. In France, for example, cities added sporting events, refreshments, and bright lights to parks and public spaces and began to call them pleasure gardens. In Britain, taverns and inns grew into pleasure gardens as owners added **landscaping**, other structures, theater, concerts, and even fireworks.

In 1661, New Spring Gardens in London, England, was one of the first pleasure gardens to become internationally famous. In 1728, the name was changed to Vauxhall Gardens. It had garden walks, mazes, shops, food, music, dancing, and sports. Millions visited this popular pleasure garden through the centuries. In 1859, Vauxhall Gardens closed with a spectacular fireworks display that spelled out "Farewell Forever!"

An open gathering area called Le bal Mabille in Paris, France, 1850

pleasure garden: a garden open to the public that offers entertainment.

world fair: an international exhibition of technology, science, and culture.

resort: a place that is a popular destination for vacations.

boardwalk: a walkway along a beach or waterfront, typically made of wood.

landscaping: an area of land with special features, such as pools and gardens.

WORDS TO KNOW

Russian Mountain: a wooden hill structure covered in ice that riders slid down in wooden sleds.

ancestor: an earlier form from which something modern has developed. Also a person from your family or culture who lived before you.

exhibition: a public show of art or other interesting things.

technology: the tools, methods, and systems used to solve a problem or do work.

innovative: coming up with new ideas or methods of doing things.

Pleasure gardens didn't have rides (yet), but some rides, such as the roller coaster, got their start around the same time. Eventually, these rides became part of the parks and gardens.

Built in 1583, **BAKKEN**, in Denmark is claimed to be the oldest amusement park.

RUSSIAN MOUNTAINS

Perhaps the Russians were developing the first kind of amusement park ride when they built their famous slides. As early as the fifteenth century, the Russians created huge ice slides for fun. Called **Russian Mountains**, these were manmade wooden hills covered with ice. Children and adults climbed 70-foot staircases to reach to the top. Then, the riders slid down the mountain in wooded sleds that could reach 50 miles per hour! Does this sound like the kind of ride you might encounter at an amusement park?

The first modern roller coaster—the Promenades Aeriennes—opened in Paris in 1817. The coaster included wheeled cars instead of sleds. The wheels locked to the track, allowing the ride to go faster more safely.

Russian Mountains are thought to be the **ancestors** of the modern roller coaster. By the early 1800s, Russian Mountains started popping up in pleasure gardens all around Europe. They weren't very safe, though. No helmets, no safety barriers, and no brakes! In 1817, the owner of two Russian Mountains in Paris decided to improve the rides by adding locking wheels to the sleds. This way, riders at least had a shot of stopping when they wanted to.

In 1950, **WALT DISNEY** (1901–1966) visited Tivoli Gardens in Copenhagen, Denmark. This early amusement park changed Disney's concept for **DISNEYLAND.**

WORLD FAIRS

World fairs are large international **exhibitions**. They began in the mid-nineteenth century and were a chance for countries to show off new **technology,** such as new kinds of tools, **innovative** architecture, and special inventions—even the telephone.

FAIRGROUND PHYSICS

Several countries, including France and Britain, held large exhibitions in the seventeenth and eighteenth centuries. But the first modern international fair was held in London in 1851. It was called the Crystal Palace Exhibition. This first world fair showed off scientific and technological wonders from all around the world. The Crystal Palace was such a success that more than 40 world fairs were held between 1880 and the beginning of World War I (1914–1918).

The **EIFFEL TOWER** was built for the 1889 **EXPOSITION** in Paris.

Many technologies shown at world fairs eventually became amusement park rides. For example, the 1876 Centennial Exposition in Philadelphia, Pennsylvania, featured a **monorail**. This was intended to demonstrate a new form of mass transportation. Later, the monorail became a **staple** of amusement parks. Have you ever been to Disney World and ridden the monorail? You can thank the 1876 Centennial Exposition!

The exposition also introduced a steam-powered elevator that took passengers to the top of a 300-foot tower. After the fair, the ride was taken to Coney Island in New York and renamed the Iron Tower.

Queen Victoria (1819–1901) opening the 1851 Crystal Palace Exhibition in London

The Midway

The **midway** got its start as the "Midway Plaisance" at the 1893 World's Fair in Chicago, Illinois. Back then, the term referred to the entire amusement area. This name distinguished it from the other, more serious areas of the exposition. As amusement parks grew into their own, the midway came to mean the area of the park with food, games, sideshows, arcades, fun houses, **souvenir** booths, and small rides, such as the bumper cars. The midway also forms the main path people use to travel through the park.

Another, more well-known ride got its start at the 1893 World's Fair in Chicago—the Ferris wheel. Before this, upright wheel rides were called **pleasure wheels**, and they'd actually been around for centuries. But the planners of the Chicago exposition wanted something spectacular to rival the Eiffel Tower, which Paris had built for the 1889 exposition. So, they hired George Washington Gale Ferris Jr. (1859–1896) to design a huge pleasure wheel.

Ferris's wheel—the first and only one he ever designed—was 250 feet in diameter. The wheel had 36 **gondola** cars that could hold 60 people each. Ferris's wheel could carry 2,160 people at one time! His wheel made such a big impression that all pleasure wheels are called Ferris wheels now.

A traveling Englishman sketched an early **FERRIS WHEEL** in Bulgaria in 1620.

The first Ferris wheel. Does it look much different today?

WORDS TO KNOW

concessions: an area for selling food and drinks at a fair or amusement park.

trolley: a small train powered by electricity from an overhead cable. Also called a cable car.

Actually, the whole 1893 Chicago world fair was organized around the Ferris wheel. It sat in the center of a midway with **concessions** all around it. Sound familiar? The layout of the Chicago World's Fair was so successful that future amusement parks in America copied the midway idea. In fact, the fair heavily influenced a Coney Island amusement park owner, among others.

The Sideshow

In the early days of amusement parks, sideshows ruled the midway. These were small acts that visitors paid separately to see. Acts included people who were different in some way, such as the bearded lady, the tattooed man, or the dog-faced boy. Parks prided themselves on collecting the most unusual human performers. For instance, from 1911 to 1929, Samuel Gumpertz

A sideshow tent at a circus, 1930s

(1868–1962) ran numerous sideshows on Coney Island. His most famous show was a half-sized village where 300 little people from all across the world lived. As society became more aware about what is hurtful and offensive, these acts died out. Many early amusement parks also included fun houses. A fun house is a building that includes mazes, mirrors, slides, slanted floors, spinning seats, and other fun challenges for people to navigate. Haunted houses are a type of fun house.

RESORTS, PICNIC GROVES, AND BOARDWALKS

While American amusement parks were greatly influenced by world fairs, they physically grew out of established vacation spots. These included resorts, picnic groves, and seaside boardwalks. At first, most resorts in the United States catered to wealthy vacationers. They were the only people who could afford to travel. Then, in the nineteenth century, railroads made resorts accessible to the middle class. Resorts built hotels and other amusements such as dancing, bowling, and shooting to get people to stay longer.

In the 1880s, for instance, the owner of an orchard on an island in the Ohio River opened his land to picnickers. He added amusements—including bowling and dancing—and then rides. It became a full-fledged amusement park called Cincinnati's Coney Island. Though it closed briefly in the 1970s, this small amusement park is still open—although most of its rides were moved to nearby King's Island in the 1970s.

Today, **KING'S ISLAND** is one of the largest amusement and water parks in the **MIDWEST.**

By the end of the nineteenth century, most bigger cities in the United States had **trolleys**. People used this form of transportation to commute to work and school during the week. However, not as many people used the trolleys on the weekends. Therefore, the trolley companies began building amusement parks, also called trolley parks, at the end of their lines. These parks were usually on the outskirts of town. Trolley parks encouraged people to use the trolleys on the weekends and in the evenings. The best known trolley park is Coney Island outside New York City.

Coney Island, c. 1912

WORDS TO KNOW

psychological: relating to or affecting the mind.

hormone: a chemical that carries signals from one part of the body to another.

Amusement park **DESIGNERS** often use **psychological** tricks to make rides seem more dangerous. Dark tunnels. Creaky or rickety-sounding tracks. Low overhangs that seem to just miss us. They all build up the fear and help pump **FEEL-GOOD** hormones into our brains!

Coney Island was created as a resort and, later, trolley park for New York City. After the Civil War, people began investing in this stretch of beach south of the city. At first, they built hotels, bathhouses, casinos, and racetracks. Later, they built rides. Eventually, Coney Island became a series of separate amusement parks in the twentieth century. Have you ever been?

THEME PARKS

In 1955, Walt Disney opened a themed amusement park near Los Angeles, California. Disneyland had distinct areas where the rides, food, buildings, and other features all reflected a certain theme. When Disneyland opened, it had themed areas such as "Main St USA," "Fantasyland," "Frontierland," "Adventureland," and "Tomorrowland." Adventureland, for instance, had a jungle theme, while Fantasyland was devoted to Disney's cartoon characters. Disneyland proved immensely popular and, in 1971, Disney opened Disney World near Orlando, Florida.

Today, the United States has more than 600 amusement parks, big and small, as well as a vast number of carnivals and fairs. And amusement parks have spread across the world. In 2018, more than half a billion people visited the most popular theme parks in the world! That's roughly 7 percent of the world's population. Each of these places has thrilling rides, interesting food, music, and lights—all of which we'll be exploring in this book.

ESSENTIAL QUESTION

Do people love carnival rides today for the same reasons they loved them in the last century?

DESIGN YOUR OWN
AMUSEMENT PARK

Early amusement park designers were influenced by world fairs, European pleasure gardens, and other entertainments. Designers spent many hours drawing up plans of the space and deciding what elements would go where to ensure everything fit in a way that was inviting and fun. Think about your favorite amusement park, carnival, or fair. What do you love about it? What do you not like? This is your chance to design your own. You'll be creating a map that shows your amusement park layout, features, and rides.

> Draw a map of your park on posterboard or a large sheet of craft paper. Be sure to include these elements:

* A name for your park!

* Rides, shows, and games

* Concessions and shops

* Bathrooms, first aid stations, and offices

* Connecting paths and walkways

* Water features such as ponds, streams, and rivers

* Parking

* Greenery

People have been enjoying amusement parks since before you were born! **Here's video proof from 1920s Coney Island!**

🔎 1920s Coney Island rides video

PS

> Describe each of your rides in your notebook. What would you call each of them? What kind of ride is it? Do you have a big attraction, such as a roller coaster?

Try This!

Give your amusement park a theme! You could devote the rides and overall design to your favorite book or movie, for instance.

POPSICLE
FERRIS WHEEL

George Ferris Jr. designed a giant wheel for the Chicago World's Fair. His Ferris wheel could carry more than 2,000 people at a time. This was the first and only wheel he designed! For this activity, you'll be building your own Ferris wheel.

❯ **First, build the outside of the wheel.** You'll make two **hexagons** out of triangles of craft sticks. (Tip: use the dyed ones!)

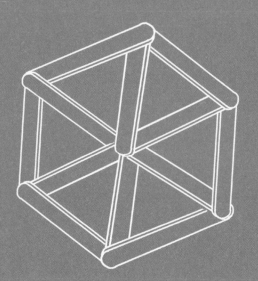

1. Arrange three popsicle sticks into a triangle and glue the ends together.

2. Add two more sticks to form another triangle. Glue.

3. Repeat this until you have a hexagon.

4. Make another hexagon the same way.

❯ **Next, join the two hexagons with popsicle stick crossbars.**

1. Break three popsicle sticks in half. These are the crossbars. Make sure they're all equal in length.

2. Lay one of the hexagons flat.

3. Glue a crossbar vertically to the center of one of the six sides of the hexagon.

4. Repeat for each crossbar. Let dry.

5. Glue the other hexagon to the crossbars. Let dry.

❯ **Now, make the supports for the Ferris wheel.** You'll need two, one for each side.

1. Make a large triangle using two popsicle sticks per side.

2. Overlap the top two sticks to create an X at the top. Glue together.

3. Repeat for the other support.

4. Add crossbars using full-size popsicle sticks between the supports. (Tip: Glue these to the bottom of the triangles so that the support will sit flatly on a table.)

To put the Ferris wheel all together, you'll need a thin wooden skewer or an unfolded paper clip.

1. Thread the skewer through the center of the Ferris wheel. This will give it something to spin around on the stand.

2. Place the Ferris wheel in its stand with the skewer resting on each X. Spin!

Try This!

Make a huge one! You can double or triple the number of popsicle sticks used to make the wheel and supports.

Do You Love the Thrill?

Many people love the feeling they get from a roller coaster barreling around a tight turn or from a drop ride plunging hundreds of feet. They feel the fear—while knowing they're safe—and it actually makes them feel great after a ride. This is due to chemistry! When we are afraid, our hearts pound, we breathe a bit faster, and we even have more energy. This is our **fight-or-flight response**. If we were really in danger, we would need to be ready to either fight or run! Our bodies produce a chemical called **adrenaline** to cause this response. When our bodies feel this rush from the adrenaline, other "feel-good" chemicals also kick in. So after a ride, we usually feel really good!

Some people adore scary activities. They might love climbing mountains, snowboarding, mountain biking, or other potentially dangerous sports. We even might call them adrenaline junkies! However, not everyone enjoys feeling fear or taking risks. Other people hate risks and avoid them at all costs. Most people, though, fall somewhere in between. And amusement parks give us a safe place to enjoy being scared.

WORDS TO KNOW

hexagon: a shape with six equal sides.

fight-or-flight response: the brain's response to defend itself against or flee from a perceived threat.

adrenaline: a hormone produced in high-stress situations. Also called epinephrine.

21

DESIGN YOUR OWN
RIDE

You just designed your own park. Now, you get to design one of the rides for the park! Think about your favorite rides. How would you make them better? Do they need to be more thrilling? Or perhaps you have an idea for a brand-new ride. Put your engineering skills to work to come up with an incredible design.

❱ **Decide on the type of ride you're designing.** Is it a roller coaster, a haunted house, a new kind of Ferris wheel?

❱ **Do a little research on that type of ride.** Most amusement parks have websites with photos or videos of their rides. You can also find many YouTube videos of amusement park rides. What features do you want your ride to have? Jot these down in your notebook.

❱ **Describe and sketch your ride in your notebook.** Tweak your design as you think of new things to add to make it more exciting. What about safety features? Don't forget to keep your riders safe!

❱ **Draw a poster advertising the ride!** You can use poster board and markers or whatever medium you like.

Do your caregivers like the same kinds of amusement park rides as you? **Maybe not! Find out why in this video.**

🔎 ABC dad wild park ride

Try This!

Make the ride fit a theme! Do you love Harry Potter or the Avengers? How can you create a park around those characters?

Chapter 2

MAKE SOME
MOTION

Bumper cars glide across the rink, slamming into each other. You steer your bumper car toward your brother's car and hit the "gas" pedal. You zoom toward him. But, just before you get there, another car rams into the side of yours. Your car goes careening in a new direction. The other car bounces away in the opposite direction. Everyone laughs as they steer, slam, and bounce around the ride.

ESSENTIAL QUESTION

How do bumper cars move? Why do they bounce?

Bumper cars are fun for almost any age—but did you know they are also the perfect way to learn about motion? Everything happening in the bumper car rink is following the laws of motion, discovered by a scientist more than 300 years ago!

WORDS TO KNOW

circuit: the complete path traveled by an electric current.

conductive: describes a material or object that allows electricity or heat to move through it.

insulator: a material that allows little or no heat, electricity, or sound to go into or out of something.

patent: a document from the government that gives an inventor the exclusive right to make, use, or sell his or her invention.

speed: the distance an object travels in a unit of time.

velocity: a measure of an object's speed and direction.

acceleration: the rate at which the speed of a moving object changes through time.

HOW THEY WORK

Bumper cars run on electricity. In fact, the whole rink is one big electrical **circuit**! On most models, the big pole rising out of the back of each car connects to an electrical ceiling grid. Metal pins on the bottom of the car connect to a **conductive** floor. This completes the electrical circuit.

When the ride operator turns the ride on, electricity flows to the bumper car motors, allowing them to run. You control the speed and direction through the pedal on the floor and the steering wheel.

Newer designs have gotten rid of the rod and the ceiling grid. Instead, the floor is made up of alternating strips of conductive and **insulator** material. That is, the conductive strip lets electricity flow, but the insulator does not. The bumper car is always in contact with each kind of strip, which means an electrical circuit is always maintained and the car can move.

History of Bumper Cars

The question of who invented the bumper car is still being debated. Some experts claim Victor Leland, a General Electric engineer, invented it. Others say that the Stoehrer brothers did. The Stoehrer brothers were the first to **patent** bumper cars, in December 1920. They started a company called Dodgem. The ride quickly became a staple at most amusement parks and fairs. By the 1970s, Dodgem was in financial trouble and sold to another company. But bumper cars live on!

MOTION

Bumper cars are all about motion. Even as the technology of bumper cars gets better and the bumper cars get more fun, they still have to follow the rules of motion.

Check out this video to learn more about how bumper cars work!

🔍 concerning reality bumper cars

PS

In that first scenario in the bumper cars on page 23, you experienced Newton's three laws of motion. We'll learn more about these laws soon, but first, what is motion? It's simply the act of an object changing position as time passes. The bumper car moves from point A to B in a couple of seconds. We can talk about and measure its motion using terms such as **speed**, **velocity**, and **acceleration**.

Originally, **BUMPER CARS** were not designed to hit one another. You were supposed to **DODGE** the other cars. That's why the first bumper car company was called **DODGEM!**

Speed is how fast the bumper car moves from A to B. We figure this out by dividing the distance the car travels by the time it takes to travel it. For example, if the car covers 5 feet in 5 seconds, you're traveling at a rate of 1 foot per second!

WORDS TO KNOW

mass: the amount of material that an object contains.

interact: how things that are together affect each other.

inertia: the tendency of an object to resist a change in motion. An object in motion tends to stay in motion and an object at rest tends to stay at rest.

Velocity is a word we sometimes use when we really mean speed. But velocity actually describes an object's speed *and* direction. Let's look at your bumper car again. Your bumper car might be traveling at a speed of 1 foot per second, but it's also moving west. This means the car's velocity is 1 foot per second west.

Acceleration describes how the car's motion changes. We can accelerate the car by changing its speed or direction—or both! In other words, the bumper car can go faster or slower, head off in a different direction, or both at the same time.

Remember, if you change either the speed or direction, this is called velocity. Acceleration is the rate at which the velocity changes. You feel acceleration when the bumper car speeds up, changes direction, or both. You can also feel acceleration when you fall! We'll get into that in Chapter 3.

Newton's Laws of Motion

1. An object stays at rest or in motion until acted upon by a force.

2. The acceleration of an object is dependent upon both the force acting upon the object and the **mass** of the object.

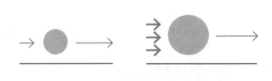

3. Whenever two objects **interact**, the force exerted on one object is equal and opposite in the direction of force exerted on the other object.

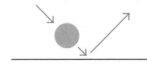

NEWTON'S FIRST LAW OF MOTION

More than 300 years ago, Sir Isaac Newton came up with three laws to describe motion. Newton's first law of motion states that an object stays at rest or in motion until acted upon by a force. A force is a push or a pull on an object.

Imagine sitting in the bumper car. It stays still until you either put your foot on the pedal—or until another car hits it. Both actions apply a force to the car. The car will stay in motion, going the same speed and in the same direction, until another force acts on it. Likewise, your bumper car will keep going in a straight line until another force acts upon it. You could tap the gas pedal, steer the car in a new direction, or another car could hit you. (It is bumper cars!) Newton called this tendency to either stay still or in straight-line motion **inertia**.

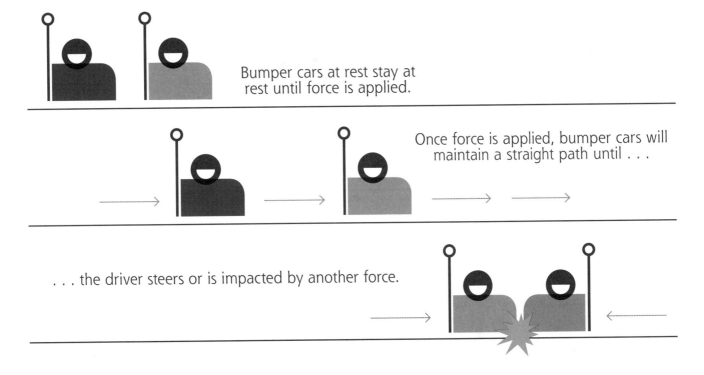

Bumper cars at rest stay at rest until force is applied.

Once force is applied, bumper cars will maintain a straight path until . . .

. . . the driver steers or is impacted by another force.

friction: the force that slows a moving object or objects when they move against each other.

proportional: corresponding in size or amount to something else.

inversely: when something increases in relation to a decrease in another thing or vice versa.

The force needs to be enough, though, to overcome the car's inertia. That is, the force needs to be great enough to make your bumper car change speed or direction. For example, imagine there are many different sizes of bumper cars zipping around the rink. If a small one hit your normal-sized one, the force might not be great enough to change your motion. Instead, the smaller one might bounce off!

What happens if the bumper car never gets hit by another car? Will it have slowed and stopped by the time it reaches the far wall? What if the arena is enormous? It's likely you won't crash into the far wall even if no one hits you again, because there is another force acting on your car—**friction**.

Friction is the resistance that a surface meets when it moves over another surface. Friction can exert a force against an object. Think of a ball rolling across carpet. Now think of that same ball rolling across a smooth wooden floor. Which goes faster? A ball rolls more slowly over a rough surface than it does a smooth one.

Bumpers Make All the Difference

The bumpers on bumper cars are made of a bouncy material. Like a ball, the bumpers give a little and then spring back when they hit something. This is called an elastic collision. The two bumper cars bounce off each other.

Most collisions, though, aren't elastic. Think about what might happen if the cars didn't have bumpers. When they hit, the cars would still move each other in equal and opposite directions, depending on their masses and speed. But the cars might also dent each other, lock together, or even flip. Two harder objects hitting each other is an inelastic collision.

Check out this bumper car simulation that lets you vary the mass, velocity, and bounciness of the cars when they hit. What happens?

Learner bumper car simulation

A roller coaster wheel generates friction when it glides over its track. If the track is smooth, the coaster will go faster. And the bumper car? As the car rolls on the floor, friction occurs between the wheels and floor, and the car eventually slows and stops.

NEWTON'S SECOND LAW OF MOTION

Bumpers cars on cruise ships run on BATTERIES. That way the cruise ship doesn't need a special rink.

Newton's second law of motion says the acceleration of an object is directly **proportional** to the net force acting on it and **inversely** proportional to the mass of the object. Remember that acceleration is a change in speed, direction, or both. That's a mouthful, but it just means that an object's change in velocity depends on how big the force is and how heavy the object itself is.

If you hit an object with a lot of force, it's going to move faster. And a heavier object is harder to move.

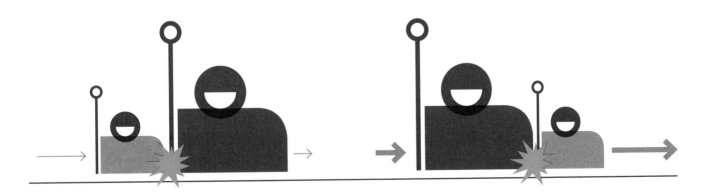

WORDS TO KNOW

momentum: a force that keeps an object moving after it has begun to move.

spectrum: a band of colors that a ray of light can be separated into to measure properties of the object, including motion and composition. Plural is spectra.

particle: a tiny piece of matter.

According to myth, **NEWTON DISCOVERED GRAVITY when** an apple hit him in the head. However, there's **NO EVIDENCE** that the apple actually hit Newton while he sat under the tree. Why do you think stories that aren't true persist through history?

Imagine your bumper car is moving slowly north. Then, a fast-moving car smacks into you from behind. Your car will speed up. The same thing would happen if a much heavier car smashed into you from behind. However, what do you think would happen if a smaller or slower car taps yours? Perhaps your car won't have as much of a reaction. But the other car might slow down or bounce off in the opposite direction—which leads us to Newton's third law of motion.

NEWTON'S THIRD LAW OF MOTION

Newton's third law states that whenever two objects interact, the force exerted on one object is equal and opposite in the direction of force exerted on the other object. In other words, if two bumpers cars hit each other, they bounce off in opposite directions. If they hit with the same force, that force will move both cars equally but in opposite directions. If the force isn't equal, one car will move a bit more and the other a bit less.

MOMENTUM: MASS IN MOTION

You've probably heard the term before. Sportscasters talk about how the football team's **momentum** makes them unbeatable. You might have heard someone say that a snowball rolling downhill picks up momentum. This means its motion seems unstoppable.

In physics, momentum is the amount of motion an object has. Momentum depends on the mass and velocity of the object. The more mass or velocity an object has, the more momentum it has. Multiplying mass times velocity gives you momentum. The equation used to figure out momentum is:
momentum = mass x velocity or
P = mv.

What is the **MOMENTUM** of
any object that isn't moving? Zero!

Thanks, Newton!

Sir Isaac Newton was a British physicist and mathematician. He is famous for discovering his three laws of motion and he was also the first to explain gravity. Newton made fundamental discoveries about light, theorizing that light is made up of all the colors in the **spectrum** and that light consists of **particles**. He wrote a momentous book called the *Principia* that laid the groundwork for modern physics. Newton is widely considered one the greatest scientists of all time.

Plus, momentum typically includes a direction—remember, velocity has direction! For example, your bumper has momentum as you skid westward across the rink. If the bumper car weighs 200 pounds and it's moving ½ mile an hour, its momentum would be 100 pounds per mile per hour westward.

Why do we care about momentum?

WORDS TO KNOW

conservation: in physics, when certain physical properties do not change in a physical system. For example, momentum isn't lost or created when two objects hit each other.

impulse: the force and time that transfers momentum from one object to another.

Remember Newton's third law? It says that when two forces collide, there's an equal and opposite reaction. This is true of their momentum, too. When a bumper hits another bumper, their momentum will be equal and opposite. And overall, the amount of momentum they share will be the same. One bumper car might gain some momentum, but the other car will lose the same amount.

Physicists call this **conservation**. That is, between the two bumper cars, they can't lose or create more momentum! This is the law of conservation of momentum. It states, "The total momentum of a group of interacting objects remains the same in the absence of external forces."

In other words, the **MOMENTUM** remains the same between the two cars unless another car hits them— and it will. What do you think would happen to the momentum if several bumper cars hit each other all at once?

Bumper cars hit each other with some force during the time they're in contact. This is called **impulse**. The impulse depends on the force and the time of the hit. Imagine one bumper car moving to the right hits a car sitting still or moving to the left. The first car transfers momentum to the second one, sending it to the right. Likewise, the second car transfers its momentum to the first car, either sending it to the left or taking away some of its momentum to the right.

Since impulse depends on both force and time, you can get the same impulse if you vary the force and time. For example, the first car could hit the other one hard but for a short amount of time.

Check out this new kind of bumper car—bumper cars on ice!

🔎 Providence bumper cars

This bumper car ride in Pripyat, Ukraine, was abandoned in 1986 after a nearby Chernobyl nuclear disaster.

Varying the IMPULSE is one of the reasons bumper cars have big rubber bumpers. The bumpers ABSORB a lot of the FORCE by slowing the time of contact between the two cars.

Or the car could hit the other one with medium force for a medium amount of time—or light force for a long time. You'll get to play with this concept in one of the activities!

Bumpers cars are a great way to explore Newton's three laws of motion. The cars are designed to collide with each other without much danger or damage. You can see what happens when a force hits a car at rest or in motion. Most of all, though, you can see that every action has an equal but opposite reaction when bumper cars slam into each other!

Newton's laws are all based on forces and how they work. You know a great way to learn about different types of force? Carnival rides that leave your stomach behind! We'll explore these rides in the next chapter.

ESSENTIAL QUESTION

How do bumper cars move? Why do they bounce?

DIY
NEWTON'S CRADLE

PHYSICS KIT
° shoebox
° string
° marbles
° glue

A Newton's cradle is a fun contraption that demonstrates
Newton's laws—as well as the law of conservation of momentum. You often see
them in offices on desks in front of bored grownups! In a Newton's cradle, a set of
balls bump into each other much like bumper cars. Store-bought cradles usually have
five metal balls suspended on wires or threads from a wooden frame. You're going to
make your own!

First, create a frame out of a shoebox.

❯ **Remove the lid from a small shoebox and set it aside.** If the lid is attached, you can
carefully cut it off.

❯ **On one side of the box,** draw a line 1 inch from the top of the box. Repeat this for the
sides and bottom. You should end up with a rectangle! Cut away this rectangle, leaving the
1-inch frame around the side. Repeat this for each side of the box. Now you should have a
cardboard frame. Depending on the type of shoebox you're using, you might need to use
some tape to hold it together so it's sturdy!

❯ **Next, you will attach
the marbles to the
strings, which will hang
in the cradle.** The marbles
should hang about two-
thirds of the way between
the top and the bottom
of the box. Measure this
height.

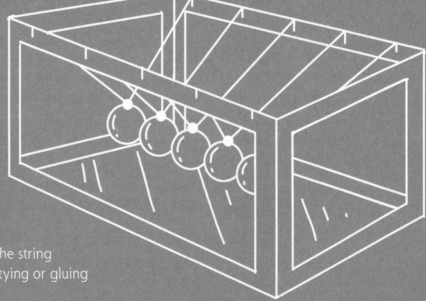

❯ **Cut six strings that are
a little more than twice this
length.** You'll be doubling up the string
to attach the marbles and then tying or gluing
the strings to the frame.

▶ **Fold one string in half** and hot glue a marble to its center.

▶ **Tie the end of each string to the frame,** one on each side.

▶ **Repeat these steps for all of the strings.** The marbles should be touching, so you may need to move the strings around.

▶ **Make sure the marbles are arranged in a straight line.** They should be the same height from the bottom and the same distance from each side. Adjust the strings and then glue their ends to the box frame.

▶ **Pull one marble back and let it go!** What happens? Draw a sketch in your science notebook.

Check out an enormous Newton's cradle!

🔎 Myth Busters
Newton's cradle

Try This!

Experiment with lifting two or more at a time. Vary the impulse at which they hit!

DIY
MINI-BUMPER CARS

Bumper cars are staples of state fairs, carnivals, and amusement parks. However, you don't need a fancy bumper car rink to make your own. You can transform a toy car (or a remote control one) into a bumper car. Tip: This will be easier to construct with a car that's at least 6 inches long.

❯ Measure the length of the car from bumper to bumper. Add about ½ inch. This will be the **diameter** of the circle you make in the next step.

❯ Draw a circle with the above diameter on a piece of cardboard. For instance, if the length of your car measured 7½ inches long, the diameter of the cardboard circle will be 8 inches.

❯ Cut out the circle.

❯ Inflate a long, thin animal balloon so that it wraps around the circle. Depending on the size of your car and the balloons, you may need several balloons.

❯ Glue the balloon around the outside edge of the cardboard circle. This is your bumper!

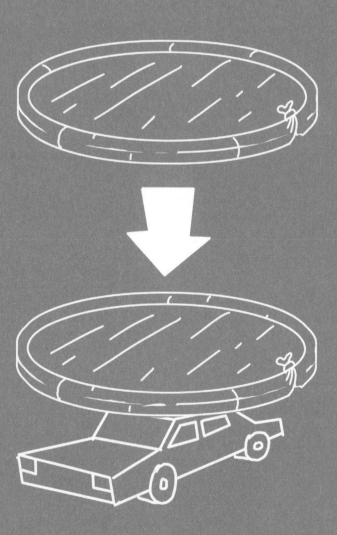

> **Place the circle atop your toy car** so that the balloon forms a bumper around the car. Its wheels shouldn't touch the balloon. Depending on the design of the car, you may need to raise the circle up a bit. You can do this by cutting out small pieces of cardboard and gluing them to center of the circle where it will attach to the car. Once you have the bumper adjusted correctly, glue or tape the inside center of the circle to the top of the car. Let dry.

> **Repeat this for the other car.**

> **Now you have two bumper cars and are ready to experiment!** What do you think will happen if your ram the two cars together head-on at the same speed? Write down your prediction in your notebook. Now try it with your bumper cars! What happens?

> **Try a few more experiments!** What if one is going faster than the other? What if you add some weight to one? Note that your bumper cars won't be able to move freely in all directions since they have wheels. How might that affect your results?

Did you know there is a 100-mile-per hour bumper car? **Watch the world's fastest bumper car break the Guinness World Record for speed!**

🔎 100 mile per hour bumper car

PS

Try This!

Make bumper boats! You can use toy boats or remote control ones. How do your results differ? Why?

WORDS TO KNOW

diameter: a straight line running from one side of a circle to the other through the center.

INERTIA
MAGIC TRICK

Some carnivals and fairs feature magicians! Have you ever seen a magician pull a tablecloth right out from under dishes? Well, they are actually doing the trick using physics rather than magic. The objects on the table have inertia. That is, they want to stay put unless there's a force that pushes or pulls them. If you tug on a tablecloth slowly, you pull the dishes with it. Give it a try!

▶ Lay a sheet of paper on a desk or table. This works better with paper that is shiny and smooth rather than with paper that is rough.

▶ Place something somewhat heavy—but not breakable—on it. Tip: Choose an object for this experiment that won't roll!

▶ Pull the paper slowly. What happens? The object probably came with the paper, right?

▶ Now pull the sheet of paper away as quickly as you can. This might take a little practice. You should eventually be able to snatch the paper away without moving the object.

Watch some science magic in this video! What made it possible for this trick to work?

🔍 Spangler TV tablecloth

PS

Try This!

Why does this trick work? Inertia keeps the item in place. But there's also friction between the paper and the object. When you pull the paper slowly, you've haven't applied enough force to overcome this friction. So, the friction acts on the object, making it move along with the paper. But when you pull the paper quickly, you've applied enough force to overcome the friction—and the object's inertia keeps it in place. Experiment with different materials. Can you perform the trick with a piece of fabric such as a kerchief? What happens if you use a rough towel?

PLAY-DOH
CIRCUITS

PHYSICS KIT
- ° Play-Doh
- ° battery connector from a craft store
- ° LED
- ° modeling clay

Remember, bumper cars run on electricity, which can flow through many materials, forming a circuit. In newer bumper cars, the floor of the rink is made out of conductive and insulating material. You're going to experiment with both kinds. Remember, Play-Doh is conductive, while modeling clay is an insulator. Electricity can flow through the Play-Doh but not the modeling clay.

CAUTION: Have an adult help with this activity.

❯ Make two small shapes out of the Play-Doh. Place them close together but don't let them touch—yet.

❯ Snap a battery connector onto the top of the battery.

❯ Stick the positive lead (usually red) into one of the pieces of Play-Doh.

❯ Stick the negative lead (usually black) into the other piece.

❯ Separate the legs of the LED and stick one into each of the shapes. Tip: The longer leg is positive.

❯ What happens? The LED should light up. If it doesn't, flip the LED around. You have a circuit! You can put other LEDs into this circuit.

❯ Now, move the two pieces of Play-Doh together. What happens? The LED should go out. This is a short circuit!

❯ Separate the shapes again and put a piece of modeling clay between them. What happens now? The light should come back on! Why?

❯ When you push the Play-Doh together, the electricity flows from the Play-Doh to the Play-Doh and can't reach the LED. This is called a short circuit. If you put the modeling clay, an insulator, in between the pieces, this restores the flow of electricity to the LED!

Try This!

Experiment with what you can create. Make a ride that lights up! If your original design doesn't work at first, keep testing and redesigning until it does!

Chapter 3

FEEL THE
FORCE

In Chapter 2, we explored motion that happens in straight lines and talked a bit about forces, which cause things to move. A force is simply a push or pull on an object. The bumper cars pushed each other—this is called exerting a force. In a tug of war, two sides pull on the rope. They exert force. The side with the most force pulls the other side to them. But motion works in other ways, too.

Have you ever been on a fairground ride that made it feel like you left your belly behind? There are several rides that work with motion going in different directions, such as the drop tower, Gravitron, and pendulum swing. These are the rides that sometimes make people feel nauseous! Let's look at how they work.

ESSENTIAL QUESTION

What makes objects move? What is force?

THE DROP TOWER— AND GRAVITY

Time to feel some gravity! Head to the drop tower ride for a thrill. After you're harnessed into your seat, the drop tower ride slowly raises you hundreds of feet in the air. The view is spectacular— the other fair goers seem tiny below. The drop tower pauses at the top. Then . . . it lets go.

The world's tallest drop tower ride— ZUMANJARO DROP OF DOOM— reaches speeds of 90 miles per hour!

For a split second, you feel like you're floating in the air. You and your seatmates **plummet** toward the earth at 60 miles per hour or more. You feel weightless. Everyone screams! The brakes grab the ride before you hit the ground.

Sound exciting? How does the drop tower ride work? First, the ride lifts riders up into the air by pushing, or applying an upward force. When the seats are released, riders go into free fall because of gravity, the force that pulls them back to Earth. Free fall is when objects fall without another force—other than **air resistance**—pushing back.

Experience the Zumanjaro Drop of Doom at Six Flags Great Adventure.
Does it affect you even from the comfort of your screen?

🔎 Zumanjaro Drop Doom

PS

satellite: a manmade object placed in orbit in space used to gather information or to make communication possible.

atmosphere: the blanket of gases around the earth.

orbit: the path of an object circling another object in space.

fundamental: a central or primary rule or principle on which something is based.

gravitational: relating to the force of gravity.

electromagnetic: one of the fundamental forces of the universe, which is responsible for magnetic attraction and electrical charges.

weak force: a fundamental force that works inside the nucleus of an atom.

strong force: a fundamental force that works inside the nucleus of an atom.

nucleus: the central part of an atom. Plural is nuclei.

ellipse: an oval shape.

GRAVITY is always pulling at us, but usually something—such as the ground or the seat in a ride—is pushing back enough to keep us from falling.

Gravity is a pulling force that happens between all objects in the universe. Gravity depends on the mass of the object. More mass means more pull. And the biggest object on Earth is Earth itself. So, in the gravity tug of war between our bodies and the earth, the planet wins, hands down.

All smaller objects near the earth are pulled toward it. This includes **satellites**, our moon, spaceships, asteroids, and more. Some fall to Earth or burn up in the **atmosphere** as they pass through, but most go into **orbit** around the planet.

Four Fundamental Forces

There are four forces that cannot be explained in terms of another force. These are called **fundamental** forces. They are **gravitational**, **electromagnetic**, **weak**, and **strong forces**. Gravity is the force that acts between all objects in the universe. Electromagnetic forces act between the electrically charged parts of an atom. They're responsible for the structure of atoms as well as electricity and magnetism. Weak and strong forces act on a much smaller scale inside the **nucleus** of an atom. These forces are much harder to observe than gravity and electromagnetism, since they do their work at a subatomic level.

All planets orbit the sun, though their orbits are not the perfect circles shown here.

These objects go into orbit because they are traveling fast enough to keep them from falling. We'll learn more about circular motion in a bit!

The most massive object in our solar system is the sun. Its gravity pulls everything in around it, which is why all the planets orbit the sun.

Even though the MOON is 238,900 miles away, the earth tugs the moon into a **CIRCULAR MOTION** around it.

During the early 1600s, a German astronomer named Johannes Kepler (1571–1630) described how planets orbited the sun. But he didn't explain why they did this. Sir Isaac Newton wondered why the moon orbited in a circular motion around the earth. Newton theorized that some force must be causing moons to move around planets and planets to move around the sun in circles or **ellipses**.

WORDS TO KNOW

dilute: to make thinner or weaker through the addition of distance or material.

inverse square law: the principle in physics that the effect of certain forces on an object varies by the inverse square of the distance between the object and the source of the force.

space time: the concept that time and three-dimensional space act on each other and exist together in a four-dimensional continuum. Also called the space-time continuum.

constant acceleration: the steady rate at which a falling object picks up speed.

According to legend, the idea of gravity struck Newton when he was hit on the head by an apple while sitting in an orchard. Newton never wrote about this. But he did write several thought experiments as he tried to figure out what this mysterious force was and how it worked.

He concluded that two masses, such as the moon and the earth, are attracted to each other. The force between them depends on both their masses and the distance between them. The force of gravity is **diluted** by distance. In fact, the force is proportional to the inverse square of the distance. The equation for this is $F \sim 1/d2$. This is called the **inverse square law**. This means that the farther apart objects are from each other, the weaker the force will be between them.

Einstein's Gravity

In the early part of the twentieth century, physicist Albert Einstein (1879–1955) explained gravity differently than Newton did. According to Einstein, objects create gravity by curving time and space. These he saw as one "fabric" called **space time**, or the space-time continuum. Imagine a trampoline as space time. If you place a bowling ball in the middle, it will create a dip in the fabric. Smaller objects on the trampoline will be drawn to the bowling ball. For instance, if you tossed some marbles onto the fabric, they will end up circling and then coming to rest next to the bowling ball. However, if you placed a much larger object on the trampoline, the bowling ball would be drawn to it. This is how Einstein envisioned gravity working!

Want to dig a little deeper into Einstein's concept of general relativity? **Check out this video on gravity.**

🔎 PBS Gravity An Illusion

Mass vs. Weight

Many people use the terms *mass* and *weight* as if they were the same thing. They're not really! Mass is the amount of matter in an object. Weight is the mass plus the pull of gravity. On Earth, an object might weigh 100 pounds. However, in space, the object might weigh very little because there's very little gravity there. The moon's gravity is $\frac{1}{6}$ (16.6 percent) of the earth's gravity. On the moon, the object would weigh $\frac{1}{6}$ of what it does on earth, or 16.7 pounds. The object's mass doesn't change, but its weight depends on gravity!

Now that we know more about gravity, let's get back to the drop tower ride. As the tower falls, it's pulled downward by gravity. And it picks up speed as it falls—but it does so at a constant rate. This is also due to gravity. All objects in free fall experience **constant acceleration**. On Earth, that rate is 32 feet per second, or 9.8 meters per second. This rate does vary slightly from place to place on Earth due to the planet's shape and spin, but, in general, this is a good rate to use. So, the ride picks up speed at a uniform rate until it hits the ground—well, until the ride operator hits the brakes.

Unless you're in a vacuum, free fall isn't actually free. There is a force that pushes back as you fall. The air pushes back! This friction is known as air resistance. This is why a feather doesn't appear to fall at the same rate as a bowling ball. The surface of the feather catches the air as it encounters air molecules while it falls, which slows it down.

Watch a ball fall in a strobe light to see how falling objects pick up speed. How does the strobe light help with the visual?

🔎 MIT physics falling ball

On the moon, there is no atmosphere, which means it's the perfect place to do some motion experiments! **Check it out in this 1971 video.**

🔎 NASA hammer feather

The MASS of the earth is 5.972 x 10²⁴ kilograms. That's roughly 6,000,000,000,000,000,000,000,000 kilograms.

FAIRGROUND PHYSICS

THE GRAVITRON AND CENTRIPETAL FORCE

So far, we've talked about how rides work when they travel in straight lines, from bumper cars to drop towers, either on the ground or in free fall. But many, many rides actually go in circles. The carousel. Ferris wheel. Tilt-a-whirl. And the Gravitron.

From the outside, the Gravitron looks like a flying saucer. Inside, the outer walls of the ride are padded, and the ride operator sits in the middle of the saucer. Riders lean against one of the padded spots along the wall and strap themselves in. The Gravitron starts to slowly spin. At first, it feels a bit like being on a carousel. But the ride spins faster and faster. As it does, you feel your body pressed harder and harder against the padded wall until you feel like you can't move. Then, the ride gradually slows down and stops. Sound like fun?

The Gravitron
credit: Michel Curi (CC BY 2.0)

The Gravitron is using **centripetal force**. The bumper cars we studied travel in a straight line until something—a force—acts on them. If that force pulls something into a circular path, it is called centripetal force, or center seeking. That's what the Gravitron does. As the ride turns and goes faster and faster, it pulls you in a circle. If the walls weren't there to stop you, you'd go flying off in a straight line! The centripetal force would stop and you'd keep following your natural forward motion forward—until gravity pulled you downward. Not a ride you want to take!

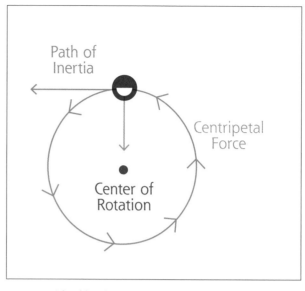

Rides like the carousel or Gravitron exert centripetal force to move in a circle

SIMULATORS **that are much like the Gravitron ride are used to simulate heavier GRAVITATIONAL FORCES.**

When you're on the Gravitron, or any other centripetal ride, you feel an outward tug—the **centrifugal force**. But it's not a real force! For instance, in the Gravitron ride, you feel like you're being pushed into the wall or your seat. But what you're really feeling is the force that the wall or seat is exerting to keep you in place.

Remember the scenario in which you are flung off the ride and kept going straight? Some people also call that force the centrifugal force. But what would really happen is that the centripetal force breaks and your body's own inertia takes over. Remember that law about objects in motion? They tend to stay in motion in the direction they were traveling. Your body continues to travel because of inertia. This sends you in the straight motion path your body wants to travel in.

Watch the Multi-Axis Trainer at Space Camp simulate what it would be like to spin in low gravity. Have you ridden fair rides like this one?

🔎 Tom Scott NASA spin

WORDS TO KNOW

radius: a straight line from the center of a circle or sphere to any point on the outer edge.

You need **MORE FORCE** to swing something in a **SMALLER CIRCLE**.

How much centripetal force do you need to move an object? That depends on its mass and acceleration. For an object traveling in a circle, its acceleration depends on its velocity and the **radius** of the circle.

All circular rides use centripetal force. They are moving riders in a circle but at different speeds and magnitudes of force. The carousel, for example, goes much slower than the Gravitron, so it exerts less centripetal force. Its riders only need to sit on a pony or hold onto a pole to keep from getting flung off. What might happen if the carousel spun really fast?

Other circular rides have several forces acting on them. The Ferris wheel experiences centripetal force and gravity. This ride rotates vertically. Centripetal force pulls the seats and riders in a circle. Yet gravity pulls riders downward, too. On the way up to the top of the wheel, the seats push the riders upward and move them in a circle. As riders head toward the bottom of the wheel, the seats and restraints keep them from both falling and being propelled forward.

History of the Carousel

Carousels have quite a long history, perhaps going back to a twelfth century training game. The word *carousel* comes from the French word for "little war." The carousel started as a practice device or training game. Legless wooden horses were hung from a rotating pole, which was turned by humans, horses, or mules. Horsemen mounted the wooden horses to practice spearing or jousting. By the nineteenth century, carousels based on the training game were appearing at European fairs to entertain civilians. According to legend, the biggest, most decorated horse on the carousel is considered the lead horse.

Though considered a kiddie ride, the teacups are great fun because they use multiple centripetal forces together. A teacup ride is really several circles spinning somewhat independently. The entire ride rotates. Groups of teacups sit on a "saucer" that rotates, too. And every teacup can spin! Riders can usually control the spin of their own teacup. So the riders get the pull of centripetal force in three ways.

The OUTER HORSES on a carousel are **FASTER** than the inner ones. In one turn, all arrive at the same time—but the outer horses had to **cover more ground.**

Sometimes, your teacup can feel like it's whipping you around, spinning extra fast for just a moment. This happens when each of the three circles are spinning you in the same direction at the same time. Imagine there's a mark on the front of the teacup, the saucer, and the ride itself. If all of these line up, the spin of the three circles are all moving in the same direction—and you've got three pulls tugging you along that line. Don't worry! This rarely happens.

Watch the mesmerizing pattern of teacups moving around and around! What pattern is it spinning in?

🔍 Kaffekoppen

PS

WORDS TO KNOW

pendulum: a weight hung from a fixed point that swings back and forth due to gravity.

arc: a section of a curve or part of a circle.

PENDULUM RIDES

So far, we've talked about objects moving in straight lines and circles. But some rides move in arcs, such as a swing or **pendulum** ride. What types of forces do those riders experience?

Like a playground swing, a pendulum ride swings riders back and forth in an **arc**. A pendulum swing has a large wheel of seats at the end of a very long and sturdy pole. You take your seat dangling from the giant wheel and strap in. The wheel is at the end of a 100-foot arm that will swing the ring of seats up in the air.

Gentle at first, the pendulum starts to swing back and forth. Gradually, the ride swings higher and higher in the air. As you reach the top of the arc, you feel like you could float out of your seat. Good thing you're strapped in! Then, you free fall back toward the ground as the pendulum swings toward the bottom. There, you feel heavier—until you begin climbing up into the sky, starting the free fall cycle all over again.

Some people get **NAUSEOUS** on **PENDULUM** rides. **MOTION SICKNESS** is caused when what you see is different from the information gathered by the mechanism in your inner ear that senses motion.

In free fall, you feel weightless, like you're floating, as you plunge back to Earth. This is the same feeling inspired by the drop rides—skydivers get that feeling, too, as do people in a plunging elevator.

As the mechanism pulls the seat upward, the seat pushes you upward, too. Your body wants to stay in place—and so does the seat. You're feeling pressure because the seat is holding you. When the mechanism releases the seat, your body experiences a split-second delay before it starts to fall, too. Then, both the seat and your body begin falling at the same rate. This creates that feeling of weightlessness.

You can also experience a brief weightless feeling on a swing. The swing follows an arc. When riders swing up to the top of the arc, they feel weightless before gravity pulls the rider and swing back down. Then, the swing rises to the top of the arc on the other side, and riders again feel momentarily weightless. Remember the delay that happens on the free fall ride? The same thing happens here, on both up sides of the arc.

Planes such as the VOMIT COMET can simulate both the GRAVITY of the moon and Mars. The plane can do this by changing the angle of the ARC it flies.

The push and pull of force make the rides at an amusement park fun—for most people. (For some, it might make them a bit queasy!) The best rides combine one or more forces, such as gravity or centripetal force, and move us in thrilling and sometimes stomach-dropping directions. As we'll see in the next chapter, the roller coaster does all this and more!

ESSENTIAL QUESTION

What makes objects move? What is force?

NASA's "Vomit Comet"

NASA uses the idea of a pendulum to train astronauts for the weightlessness of space. Astronauts train in a large plane, stripped of most of its seats. With the trainees strapped in, the plane climbs into the sky—and then dives. As it does so, the people inside unstrap—and float! Weightlessness lasts for about 25 seconds. Really, the plane and its occupants are simply falling at the same rate—but nothing is holding the people in place. As the plane levels out, its occupants do, too. Then, the plane climbs back up to repeat the process. The weightless scenes in the movie *Apollo 13* were filmed in NASA's plane. Many astronauts call it the Vomit Comet. Can you guess why?

Take a look at the Vomit Comet in action in this video.

🔍 Zero G in airplane

BALLOON
SPLAT ART

Balloons are one of the many things you can buy at fairs and carnivals. But did you know you could make art with them while exploring gravity and potential energy? You might want to do this activity outside. It can get messy.

❯ Put a teaspoon of poster or craft paint in a balloon.

❯ Fill the balloon with water.

❯ Tie the balloon off and shake it to mix the paint.

Before **RUBBER BALLOONS** were **invented, people used to inflate pig bladders** and animal intestines!

❯ Repeat these steps for the other colors you want to use.

❯ Lay the poster board or craft paper on a flat surface outside.

❯ Drop the first balloon from about 5 feet. How big a splat did it make? Let the paint dry.

❯ Vary the heights of the other balloons you drop. Do you notice a difference in the size of the splash?

❯ Which balloon had the biggest splash? Do you notice a pattern? Experiment by dropping balloons from even higher places.

WHAT'S HAPPENING?

The higher balloons should have made the bigger splats. This happens because of gravitational potential energy. When you let go of the balloon, gravity pulls it to the ground. But the balloon also has something called potential energy. As you hold it above the ground, the balloon has the potential to release energy. The higher the balloon is, the more potential it has. So, the higher object will hit the ground with more energy.

WORDS TO KNOW

bladder: a sac of tissue in the body of animals that holds urine.

MASON JAR
ACCELEROMETER

When you're using a map app or playing a game such as *Pokémon Go*, your smartphone knows which direction you're walking and how fast. It has a small device called an accelerometer. It measures your change in speed and direction—or your acceleration. If you're standing still, you are experiencing just the pull of gravity. But in a car going around a corner, for instance, or accelerating from 0 to 60, you're experiencing acceleration. We're going to build a simple accelerometer that will show you the direction and relative amount of acceleration as you walk.

CAUTION: Ask an adult to help poke the hole through the cork.

> Measure the distance between the top of the jar and the bottom.

> Cut a length of string about ½ inch shorter than this distance.

> Poke a hole in the cork and thread the string through it. Knot the string.

> Glue the other end of the string to the inside of the lid. Attach it to the center of the lid. When you close the lid, the string (with the cork) should dangle about three-quarters of the way toward the bottom of the jar.

Accelerometers

Like the one you're building, these devices measure changes in speed and direction. Once upon a time, accelerometers were rocket science. They were used only in rockets and jets. In a rocket, for instance, the accelerometer tells it how fast it's going, what direction it's pointed in, and how much gravitational pull it's experiencing. Accelerometers also help jets and airplanes **navigate**. Today, most electronic gadgets have accelerometers in them, too. They tell your phone which way is up and how fast you're moving. They also tell your game console how hard you punched or if you dodged incoming fire!

> **Fill the jar with** water and screw on the lid.

> **Turn the jar over so that it sits on its lid.** The cork should float, with the string straight up and down.

> **Now, you're ready** to experiment with your accelerometer.

> **Hold it at arm's length,** level in front of you.

> **Start walking.** Observe what happens to the cork. Does it move? In which direction? What happens if you walk faster?

> **Try walking backward.** What happens to the cork? Does its direction change? Try spinning in a circle! What happens to the cork? Why do you think this happens? Record your observations in your notebook.

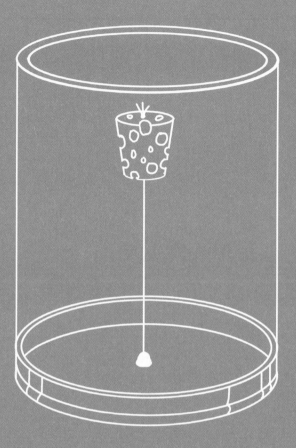

WHAT'S HAPPENING?

The cork should move in the direction of the acceleration. As you move forward, for instance, the water in the jar moves to the back of the jar, pushing the cork forward!

Try This!

Experiment with your accelerometer while you're a passenger in a car—or on a playground ride, such as the merry-go-round. What do you think will happen?

WORDS TO KNOW

accelerometer: a device that measures changes in speed and direction.

navigate: to find your way from one place to another.

DIY
PENDULUM

Pendulum rides pick up speed as the arm of the ride goes higher and higher. For this activity, we're going to build a simple pendulum and measure its speed.

❯ Tie a piece of string onto a small weight or object. This is your pendulum.

❯ Place two pieces of tape exactly a foot apart. These can be on the wall or the floor.

❯ Hold the weight exactly between these two marks. You may need another person to hold the pendulum or you can tie it to something.

❯ Bring the weight back just beyond one of the tape marks.

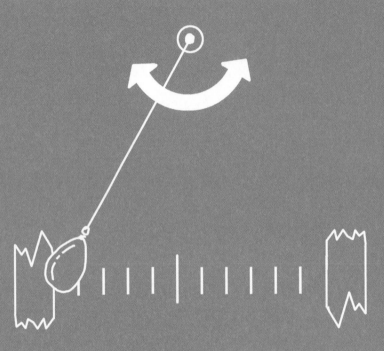

❯ Have your timer ready—and release the weight.

❯ Time how long it takes for the pendulum to swing from one piece of tape to the other.

❯ Calculate its speed by dividing the time by the distance (speed = distance ÷ time). For instance, if the pendulum took 3 seconds to go 12 inches, its speed would be 4 inches per second.

❯ Now, experiment with raising the pendulum higher and higher. Do you think it will go faster? Record your results and observations.

Try This!

Vary the weight of the object! Do heavier objects move faster? Why?

PENDULUM
PAINTING

You can create art while exploring how pendulums move. Pendulums can make fascinating patterns, depending on the force applied.

PHYSICS KIT
° large sheet of paper
° something to suspend the pendulum from
° paper cups
° string
° paints

CAUTION: You might want to do this one outside. It gets messy!

❱ **Spread a large piece** of craft paper or poster board on the ground. If you're inside, put a drop cloth or newspapers underneath.

❱ **Place a chair on either side of the paper** with a broom handle or other straight stick going across. You'll hang the pendulum from this.

❱ **Poke a small hole in the bottom of a paper or plastic cup.** Cover the hole with masking tape for now.

❱ **Poke two holes on the opposite sides of the cup near the rim.** Tie string through these holes. Hang the cup from the broom handle.

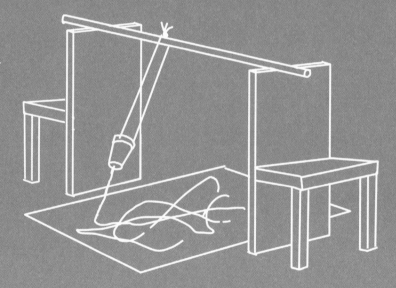

❱ **Pour a little poster paint** into the cup.

❱ **Remove the tape** and quickly set the pendulum cup in motion. It should drip paint in a pattern on the paper. You may need to experiment with the motion a bit to get a cool pattern. Let the pendulum go until it runs out of paint—or stops.

❱ **Observe what kind of pattern you created.** What happens if you swing the pendulum higher or change its direction?

Try This!

Let the paint dry. Then, fill the cup with another color and set it in a slightly different motion.

JELL-O
CENTRIFUGE

PHYSICS KIT

° 4 clear plastic cups
° string
° 2 different colors of Jell-O
° 3 marbles

Remember the Gravitron? Centripetal force moves you around in a circle. If it spins at a high enough speed, you feel pressed against the wall of the ride. In fact, that wall is keeping you from shooting out! Scientists use this same principle in centrifuges. They might spin a liquid, such as blood, to separate the denser elements, which will move to the outside of the circle. We're going to experiment with our centrifuge, spinning marbles in Jell-O!

❱ First, make a simple centrifuge. Punch two holes—one on each side near the rim—in one plastic cup.

❱ Cut a long length of string and tie each end to the holes in the cup. You now have a centrifuge!

❱ Next, prepare your Jell-O cups. Have an adult help you follow the directions on the packet.

❱ Pour the Jell-O into the other three cups, but fill them only halfway. Let the Jell-O set in the refrigerator for two hours.

❱ Once the Jell-O is set, put a marble in the center of each cup. Push it down a bit so it won't move.

❱ Make the second color of Jell-O. Pour this Jell-O into the three cups, covering the first layer and the marble. Leave some room at the top of the cup.

WORDS TO KNOW

centrifuge: a machine with a rapidly rotating container that applies centrifugal force to its contents to separate fluids of different densities or liquids from solids.

denser: more mass in the same space.

Human Centrifuge

Most space agencies and air forces use human centrifuges to train pilots and astronauts to withstand high gravitational forces—or g forces.

Here you can watch astronaut Chris Hadfield explain why! He also gives you a peek at the largest human-rated centrifuge in the world.

🔎 Chris Hadfield: Inside the Centrifuge

❯ **Let the Jell-O set** for two hours in the refrigerator. Now, we're ready to spin!

❯ **When the Jell-O is set,** place one of the cups inside the centrifuge cup.

❯ **Holding the string in the center,** swing the cups around your head 20 to 30 times.

❯ **Take the cup with the Jell-O** and marble out of the centrifuge. Examine it.

Depending on the Jell-O colors you used, you may need to shine a light through the Jell-O in order to see the marble. Did the marble move? If it didn't, the gelatin might be too firm. You can let it warm up and/or spin the Jell-O cup again harder.

❯ **Spin the other cups.** What happens? Record your observations in your science journal.

Try This!

Spin the other cups at different speeds. You might experiment with shorter and longer strings, too. Do you notice any difference?

Chapter 4

GOT
ENERGY?

Both thrill seekers and physicists love roller coasters! These rides combine force, motion, and energy. Let's try it—you jump in the first car. The safety bar clicks into place. Then, the roller coaster is slowly pulled up the first hill, the launch mechanism ratcheting as it climbs to the top. There, you catch a glimpse of the awe-inspiring view—just before the coaster begins its plunge down the hill. You throw up your hands and scream along with everyone else!

The coaster races to the bottom of the track and then hurtles up the next hill. It continues down the hill, through a twisty turn, up and down more hills, and around turns until the track brakes slow the coaster to a crawl as it comes into the station. What kinds of forces did you just experience? What made you speed up and slow down? Let's look at how roller coasters do work as well as gather and expend energy.

ESSENTIAL QUESTION

How do roller coasters get their energy?

WORK WITH PHYSICS

Let's start with how the roller coaster climbs that first hill. Its launch mechanism applies a force—either a push or pull—to move the cars up the first hill. Physicists call this **work**. Just like the term *force*, the word *work* has a special meaning in physics. It's the force applied to an object to move it across a distance. For example, if you push a block or lift a book, you're doing work. And roller coasters do work!

Like trains, roller coasters have BRAKES, but the brakes are usually built into the tracks at the end of the ride rather than on the cars.

Have you ever heard a clack-clack-clack sound as the roller coaster goes up the first hill? That's the **launch system**. Most coasters are pulled up the first hill with a chain system. A long chain or several chains run up the hill under the track. The chain is fastened in a loop to gears at the top and bottom of the hill. A motor turns the gears so that the chain moves up the hill like a long conveyer belt. The roller coaster grips onto the chain with its chain dogs. These are heavy pieces of metal underneath the coasters. The dogs release when the coaster gets to the top of the hill. If the chain breaks, anti-rollback chain dogs keep the coaster from rolling back down the hill.

catapult: a device used to hurl or launch something.

hydraulic: describes a system that pushes and pulls objects using the motion of water or other liquids.

pneumatic: describes a system that pushes and pulls objects using tubes filled with air or other gases.

mechanical energy: energy related to motion and height.

chemical energy: energy from a chemical reaction.

radiant energy: energy from light.

electrical energy: energy related to electricity.

electron: a negatively charged particle swirling around the nucleus of an atom.

nuclear energy: energy produced by a nuclear reaction, typically the splitting of an atom.

An early roller coaster in Ireland, late 1800s

Some modern coasters are using new launch systems. One kind uses electromagnets to pull the roller coaster up the lift hill. Other systems **catapult** the cars up the hill rather than pulling them. A **hydraulic** launch system, for instance, uses compressed liquid and a **pneumatic** one uses compressed air. These systems push the roller coaster cars up the hill. After that, though, the roller coaster is on its own!

Coaster tracks are **DESIGNED** to **SWAY** a couple of inches as the train goes by, especially in tight curves. If the track is too **RIGID**, it might **SNAP**!

MECHANICAL ENERGY

What gives the coaster the ability to do this work? Energy! Energy is simply the ability to do work. The launch mechanism uses mechanical or electrical energy to do the work of moving the coaster up the hill.

Forms of Energy

Energy comes in different forms, but they are all the result of the fundamental forces we learned about in Chapter 3. **Mechanical energy** comes from the motion of objects and result of gravity. For instance, the roller coaster has potential energy as it sits atop the first hill. The coaster has mechanical kinetic energy as it rolls down a hill. **Chemical energy** comes from chemical reactions. For instance, when you eat food, your body breaks it down and turns it into chemical energy. **Radiant energy** is energy that travels through space. This includes light, infrared radiation, microwaves, and much more. For example, the sunlight striking the pavement or a piece of metal at the amusement park is a form of radiant energy. **Electrical energy** comes from the **electrons** of the atom. We'll discuss this one in more detail in Chapter 6! **Nuclear energy** comes from the nucleus of the atom. Nuclear energy can be released when the atom is split. This is used for nuclear power—and nuclear weapons.

However, after launch, most coasters don't use electrical or mechanical energy to send you careening around the track. Coasters do need energy to do this, but they actually get the energy from that first hill! In all coasters, that first hill is critical. It needs to be high enough to give the coaster the energy it needs to power through all the other hills, twists, and turns without stalling out. But that hill can't be too high—otherwise, it may give the coaster too much energy, making it swerve off the track during a turn.

The **POTENTIAL ENERGY** experienced by roller coasters is really called **GRAVITATIONAL** potential energy because the energy comes from **GRAVITY**.

So, how does the coaster get energy from a hill? When the coaster sits on top of that hill, it has what we call potential energy. The object has energy because of its position. As soon as the coaster is released, gravity pulls it down the track at a constant rate of acceleration. Acceleration is calculated by dividing the change in velocity by the change in time, or $a = \Delta v \div \Delta t$.

Friction does slow the coaster a bit. Gravitational potential energy depends on the weight and height of the objects. So, if the roller coaster is sitting at 100 feet, it'll have more energy than one sitting at 50 feet. This makes the height of the first hill critical.

What happens when the roller coaster is let go atop the first hill? The coaster starts diving down the track, converting the potential energy into kinetic energy. Kinetic energy is the energy of motion. It depends on the mass of the object and its velocity. A massive coaster will have much more kinetic energy rolling down the track than would a bowling ball, for instance. So, the coaster hurtles down the first hill with a lot of kinetic energy.

Curious about how roller coasters are made? **Check out this video!**

🔎 PBS Roller Coaster STEM

PS

Then, it has to expend some of that energy to get up the next hill. The coaster has to work against inertia, gravity, and friction to climb upward along the track. But once it gets to the top of hill, the coaster has potential energy again, as well as any leftover energy from the first hill.

The process repeats itself with every hill, twist, and turn of the track until the coaster runs out of energy at the end. This flow of energy continues as the coaster travels around the track, eventually slowing to a halt (with the help of brakes) at the end of the track.

Roller coaster designers need to consider how much energy is needed from the first hill. If the hill is too steep, then the coaster might have too much energy going around a turn, causing the cars to fly off. If the hill is not steep enough, a coaster might not have enough energy to make it up a later hill or through a loop.

Coaster Brakes

Even though its cars are running out of energy by the end of the ride, roller coasters have brakes to make sure they stop precisely at the end—or in the case of emergency. The brakes are usually on the tracks rather than the cars. Most coasters have two types of brakes: trim and block brakes. The trim ones slow down the coaster in certain parts of the ride. This prevents accidents and helps build suspense. Block brakes stop the train completely.

LOOPS

Many roller coasters include loops and twists! These exert different forces than you experience on the straight pieces of track. A roller coaster loop is a lot like a spinning ride, such as a carousel or Gravitron. As you approach the loop, the coaster and your body are going in a straight line. But the track forces both to move in a circle, exerting centripetal force.

Since the loop is usually at the bottom of a hill, the roller coaster is accelerating as it enters the loop. The force of the acceleration, though, pushes you and the car downward, keeping you on the track—and in the car. (You still need your safety harness!) You feel heavier on the bottom parts of the loop because the acceleration and gravity are pulling you in the same direction.

Many roller coasters have a FRICTION WHEEL. It's a motorized wheel that controls the speed of the car through friction between the wheel and the ride.

A wooden roller coaster

Wooden vs. Steel

Originally, roller coaster tracks were made from wood—much like railroad ties on train tracks. The cars have wheels similar to trains, too. Wooden coaster tracks are supported by large frameworks of wooden or steel beams. This makes it difficult to build twists and loops. Wooden coasters are typically slower and tamer than steel ones. In the 1950s, roller coaster designers started using tubular steel tracks. The tracks are usually a pair of long steel tubes. The tracks are supported by a structure of steel tubes and beams. This framework is lightweight and sturdy, which lets designers include complex turns, twists, and loops. The cars of steel coasters can also be attached to the track in different ways. They can run over the tracks like a traditional coaster. They can be attached underneath the track. The cars can be suspended from the track above like a ski lift. The track can even be attached to the middle of the train!

As the car moves around the loop, the forces of gravity and acceleration do battle. As you head up, gravity pulls you into your seat and harness, while acceleration pushes you into the floor of the car. When you're upside down, gravity pulls you down and the acceleration pushes you up.

At the top, the forces are equal—and you'll feel light. Then, you head back down, gravity pulls you, and acceleration keeps you in your seat. By the time you level out, you feel heavy once more because both forces are going in the same direction again.

According to the Roller Coaster Database, 4,639 coasters, mostly steel, were in operation around the world as of 2018, with only **184 WOODEN** ones still running.

Just like other rides, roller coasters subject your body to acceleration and changes in force. As you plummet down a hill, you feel like you're floating—and then your stomach feels like it drops. What's happening inside you to cause this?

4-D coaster: a roller coaster where the seats are attached to the sides of the track, making riders spin and flip much more than on a regular roller coaster.

A lot of time is spent testing a NEW COASTER DESIGN to make sure it's safe! Coaster designers test their creations using WATER DUMMIES. Shaped like a human, these dummies are filled with water.

You're not solid. You have organs—like the lungs, heart, and stomach—moving inside of you. When you free fall or accelerate, your organs accelerate individually. Your stomach, for example, is free falling inside of you! Just as you feel lighter because the ride is no longer pushing on you, your stomach feels lighter because less force is pushing on it, too. When you reach the bottom of the hill and start up the next one, both you and your stomach feel that change in force!

Circular loop-the-loops can be intense. The force of the acceleration depends on the speed of the coaster and angle of the turn. To get around a circular loop, the train has to enter it going very fast. The coaster has maximum kinetic energy as it enters the loop. This gives it enough energy to make it around the whole loop. Greater speed, however, exerts greater force on the riders, making it an uncomfortable ride. So, roller coaster designers began designing teardrop-shaped loops because they required less speed.

More Dimensions

One of the newest innovations in roller coaster design is called a **4-D coaster**, or winged coaster. The seats of the coaster are attached to the sides of the track, usually two seats on each side. The seats can spin 360 degrees in a controlled way. That means, as the coaster is traveling around the track, over hills and through loops, riders are also flipping around in their own seats. Imagine all the forces acting on these riders!

Watch a demo of the 4-D roller coaster Dinoconda in China's Dinosaur Park. Would you ride one?

🔎 Official Test Run Dinoconda

Roller Coaster History

As you read in Chapter 1, roller coasters probably started off as ice hills called Russian Mountains. In warmer climates, ride operators got the idea to put wheels on the sleds. In 1817, the Russes a Belleville in Paris became the first roller coaster with rollers. The French continued to expand on the idea, adding more intricate tracks with turns. The first roller coaster in the United States was Mauch Chunk Switchback Railway in Pennsylvania, built in the mid 1800s. A former coal train, it was converted into a scenic tour with some thrills. The train took passengers up the mountain at a slow pace and then took a wild, bumpy ride back down the mountain. For 30 years, these scenic rides were very popular. And they got recreated at amusement parks. By the 1920s, wooden roller coasters were a popular attraction. Since then, technology has advanced in leaps and bounds. Wooden coasters were replaced by ones made out of steel and other materials, and the designs grew more elaborate. But the same basic principles still apply!

WORDS TO KNOW

proton: a particle in the nucleus of an atom that has a positive charge.

neutron: a particle in the nucleus of an atom that does not have a charge.

repel: to push away or apart.

static electricity: electricity that collects on the surface of something and does not flow as a current. It can cause a mild shock if you touch it.

conductor: a material through which electricity and heat move easily.

ELECTRICAL ENERGY

So far, we've talked about potential and kinetic energy. Roller coasters use—and produce—other kinds of energy, too. For example, the motor that drives a chain-driven lift hill is probably powered by electricity. So are the lights, the music, and many other things at the amusement park—and in your own home.

Electricity is a form of energy that comes from charged particles deep inside all matter. All matter is made up of atoms. All atoms are made up of particles. At the center of the atom are particles called **protons** and **neutrons**. Electrons orbit the center of the atom, called the nucleus. They have a negative electric charge, while protons have a positive one. Neutrons are neutral, hence the name!

These electrical charges interact together to produce electrical force. Think about the positive and negative sides of a magnet. If you put the positive poles together, they push each other apart. But a positive pole attracts a negative one. Electrical charges work the same way! Like magnets, positive charges **repel** positive and negative charges repel negative.

Electrons (and their charges) can be passed from atom to atom, allowing electrical current to travel. This can happen in a few ways. One is friction, which can essentially rub electrons off one material and onto another.

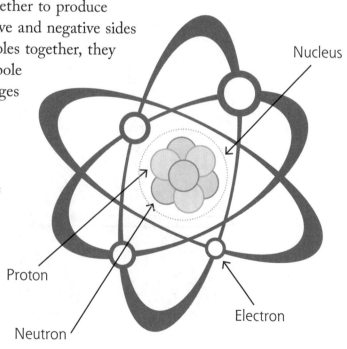

Nucleus

Proton

Neutron

Electron

Static electricity!
credit: Ingo Hoffmann (CC BY 2.0)

Have you ever shuffled your socked feet over a carpet? This friction creates and passes along an electrical charge to you, perhaps making your hair stand up or your clothes crackle. Likewise, if you rub your hair against a balloon, you create an electrical charge. The charge stays with the balloon, though. We call this **static electricity** since it doesn't move anywhere.

A CONDUCTOR is something that lets ELECTRICITY pass easily through it. That's why electrical wires are made of metal, such as copper!

Some materials are much better than others at letting electricity pass through them. If you touched something after creating static electricity, did you get a shock? If so, what did you touch? Probably something metal, right? Metals are very good **conductors** of electricity. Your body is a poor conductor!

Other materials, including plastics and wood, are not very good conductors. Electricity doesn't pass through them, so we call them **nonconductors**, or insulators. And there are some special materials—such as silicon—that can be both conductors or insulators under special conditions. These are called **semiconductors**. These are used in computer chips.

When electricity flows through a conductor, we call this an **electrical current**. To keep it flowing, there needs to be a circuit. This is the path or loop along which the electrons travel. An electrical circuit starts with a power source, such as a battery or generator. It sends electrical charge along a conductor to do work somewhere, such as turn on a light or run a motor. Then, the circuit is completed by a conductor returning to the power source.

A simple circuit might include a battery with copper wire from one terminal leading to a light bulb and then back to the battery to the other terminal. If you connect the circuit, the light turns on. This is basically what happens when the ride operator throws a switch to start the motor for the launch mechanism!

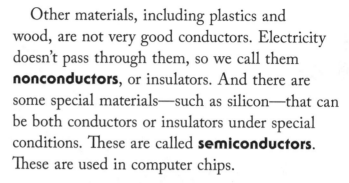

Path

Power

Switch

Load

Roller coasters are fun—for most people—because of the flow of energy up and down the hills and around the bends, twists, and loops. One thing you might want to avoid before riding a roller coaster, though, is food! And at a fairground, there is a lot of delicious food to try. Part of what makes that food so tasty is rooted in science. We'll take a look in the next chapter.

LAUNCH!

Most older roller coasters are pulled up that first hill. However, some newer coasters have pneumatic launch systems. That means a shot of compressed air launches the coaster up the hill. We're going to build a simple version of that with a straw that you blow through.

❯ Cut out a rectangular piece of paper about 6 by 3 inches.

❯ Wrap it around the base of a pencil to form a tube. Tape it together.

❯ Tape over one end of the tube, too.

❯ Draw and cut out a roller coaster car. Tape this to the closed end of the tube.

❯ Slip the open end of the tube over a straw.

❯ Blow! What happens?

❯ The coaster should fly off. The air from your lungs is pushing against the paper coaster to make it move.

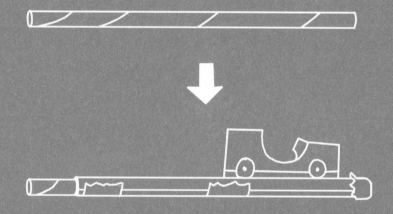

Pneumatics is being used in many different fields, including architecture and robotics! **Take a look at some of the things innovators are coming up with.**

🔎 Architecture lab pneumatic

Try This!

Experiment with the coaster design. Try making it sleeker and perhaps more rocket shaped. Does this allow the coaster to go farther? Why do you think this helps?

ROLLER COASTER
REBOOT

PHYSICS KIT
° construction paper
° marbles
° supports

In the introduction, you designed a simple roller coaster. This one will be more complex and finished. You'll get to add multiple hills, loops, twists, and turns. Plus, you'll experiment with how high to make that critical first hill.

❯ Cut several 3-inch-wide strips of construction paper. You can make them of equal length or vary the lengths. Tip: Use several different colors of construction paper.

❯ On each strip, draw a half-inch line every inch or so along both long sides of the strip. The line should be **perpendicular** to the paper.

❯ Carefully cut each of these lines. This will create a series of flaps along each side of the strip.

❯ Fold the flaps toward the center. They should now stand up to form the sides of your track.

❯ Now, you can shape your track into almost any shape: a hill, curve, straight away, twist, or loop. Start with your first hill, though.

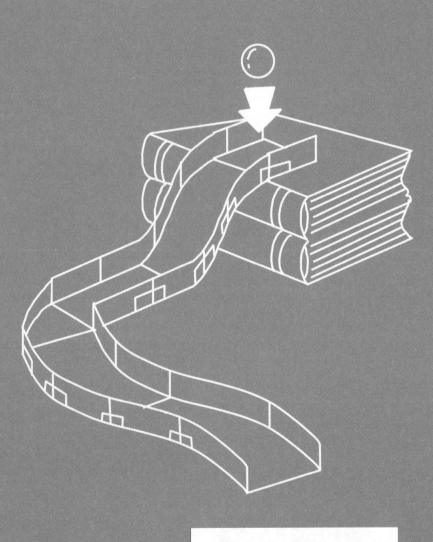

WORDS TO KNOW

perpendicular: a line at an angle of 90 degrees to another line or surface. The two lines form a corner, called a right angle.

Types of Modern Coasters

> Sit-down: riders sit inside a car.

> Stand-up: riders stand up.

> Inverted: the train is attached to the bottom of the track.

> Suspended: the cars are suspended from a swinging arm underneath the track.

> Pipeline: the track runs through the middle of the train.

> Bobsled: wheeled cars slide down a u-shaped tube.

> Flying: riders start out seated but are turned to face the ground, giving the feel of flying.

> Wing (or 4-D): two seats from each car are on either side of the track. The seats can spin or rotate.

> **Use clear tape along the flaps** to keep your track in the shape you want it.

> **Support your first hill with books or blocks.** You can tape the top of the hill to a block, for instance. Or you can build supports out of popsicle sticks!

> **Repeat the process to build new sections of your roller coaster.** Alternate colors! Add hills, twists, and loops.

> **Use clear tape** to join your sections together.

> **Test the track with a marble.** Does it make it all the way around? If not, how might you adjust the height of the first hill?

Try This!

Experiment with a very steep first hill or a very large loop! What happens? Record your observations in your science notebook.

ELECTROMAGNETIC
TRAIN

Some trains—and even some roller coaster launch systems—use a combination of electricity and magnetism to make something move. You're going to build a simple, miniature train that runs on a battery and magnets!

❯ **First, create your train.** Put a neodymium disc magnet on each end of an AAA battery. Regular magnets aren't strong enough. The magnets need to be placed on the battery with the poles facing opposite directions. Hold the magnets so that they push each other away—and then stick the battery in between. You've just made a bar magnet with a north and south pole!

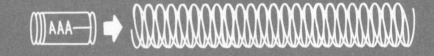

❯ **Now, create the track.** You'll need to twist some 18-gauge copper wire into a coil. Tip: Twist the copper wire around an AA battery to form the coils. That way the AAA battery will fit through the coils. You can make the track as long as you want.

❯ **To run the train,** simply stick the train (aka, the AAA battery sandwiched between the magnets) inside the copper coil. The train should zip through the coils. If it doesn't, try flipping the train around. It'll run in only one direction.

❯ **Putting the magnetic train** in the copper coil creates an electrical current that flows through the copper wire. This, in turn, creates a magnetic field right around the train, which pushes it down the track.

Try This!

Turn the coil into a closed loop. What happens? You can also experiment with using more disc magnets, if you have them.

Chapter 5

HAVE SOME
HEAT

In the last chapter, we looked at different types of energy that make a roller coaster the fun ride that it is. Heat is another type of energy. And fairs and amusement parks are not only full of heat in the summers, but there is also plenty of heat being used to make great food for visitors. Imagine funnel cake dough sizzling on the griddle. Soft-serve ice cream flowing into a warm waffle cone. Batter-dipped Oreos (or pickles!) crackling in the fryer.

ESSENTIAL QUESTION

What's the difference between heat and temperature?

Just about anything goes at a fair, from corndogs to pies on a stick. Fairgrounds and amusement parks are not only known for thrilling rides—but also yummy, and a bit unusual, food. And they all depend on heat and temperature!

FAIRGROUND PHYSICS

In this chapter, we'll explore how heat and temperature work—and how food can be fried or frozen. What's the difference between heat and temperature? Simply put, temperature describes how hot or cold something is. It's actually a measure of heat flow.

Heat is a kind of energy that moves from hot to cold temperatures. Heat is internal energy absorbed and transferred from one body to another. The process of increasing internal energy is called heating—lowering it is called cooling. So, you can heat something by applying a temperature difference so energy moves from one object to another. In this way an object gains heat energy and its temperature rises.

credit: Tony Webster (CC BY 2.0)

Temperature Scales

Through the years, scientists have devised different scales to measure temperature. In the United States, people tend to use the Fahrenheit scale, while the rest of the world uses Celsius. Daniel Fahrenheit (1686–1736) based his scale on the freezing point of sea water and human body temperature. Later, it was discovered that fresh water freezes at a higher temperature (32 degrees) and that body temperature was really 98.6 degrees. Developed by Anders Celsius (1701–1744), the Celsius scale uses equally spaced points between the boiling point of water (100) and its freezing point (0). And there's another scale! William Thomson, 1st Baron Kelvin (1824–1907), recognized the need for a temperature scale that reaches **absolute zero**, the point at which atoms stop moving. Absolute zero is the temperature at which no more energy can be taken out of an object—0 degrees Kelvin equals absolute zero.

WARMING UP

Heat can be produced from almost any form of energy. We get radiant heat from the sun. We can even get heat from mechanical energy and from friction. For example, if you were able to touch the roller coaster track after the cars have rolled over it, it would be hot. The track heats up as the coaster runs over it.

To understand heat, though, we need to back up and talk about what makes up matter itself. Matter consists of atoms. These are the smallest unit a substance can be broken down into.

Some substances are made up of only one kind of atom—we call those **elements**. However, most atoms bond with other types of atoms to form **molecules**. For example, each molecule of water is made up of one oxygen atom and two hydrogen atoms.

FAIRGROUND PHYSICS

Each molecule in a substance interacts with the others. Sometimes, they cling to each other. Others repel each other. How molecules move and interact with each other depends on the phase they're in. Matter can primarily be in three states, or phases: solid, liquid, or gas. Think about water. It can be ice, liquid water, or steam. And the difference between the three depends on temperature.

Molecules in a solid state stand still and just vibrate in place. In a liquid, molecules can rotate and roll over each other. In a gas, they're free to move around rapidly and randomly.

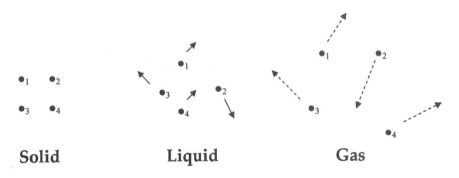

Solid   Liquid   Gas

In a solid, the molecules are closely bound together. A solid holds its shape and volume. In a liquid, the molecules are a little looser, less tightly held together. You can pour a liquid. It'll take on the shape of its container but keep its own volume. In a gas, the molecules are weakly held together. When you pump it into a container, the gas will take on the shape of the container and fill its volume.

If you put an ice cube in a warm drink, the ice cube becomes warmer, beginning to melt, and the drink becomes cooler. What's happening to create heat?

It's as though something is moving between the HOT liquid and the COLD ice cubes to even out the TEMPERATURE of the drink. HEAT is that something that flows between a lower temperature and a higher one.

Think about what happens when you rub your hands together. Do it long enough and your hands get warmer. This is due to friction. This force stretches out the molecules and causes them to snap back, releasing some energy in the form of heat. This happens when any surfaces rub together— even on the **molecular** level.

Turning up the temperature causes the molecules to move around more, rub up against each other, and release heat. If they move around enough, the molecules break their bonds to each other and the matter changes phase. Heat changes the structure of molecules in a substance. Higher temperatures change liquids into gas, for example.

Plasma is another natural state of matter. It is a high-energy, positively charged gas. It fills a container like ordinary gas does, but plasma acts very differently in other ways. Plasma isn't common on Earth, but it is common in the rest of the universe. Stars are made of plasma!

The sun is made of plasma.

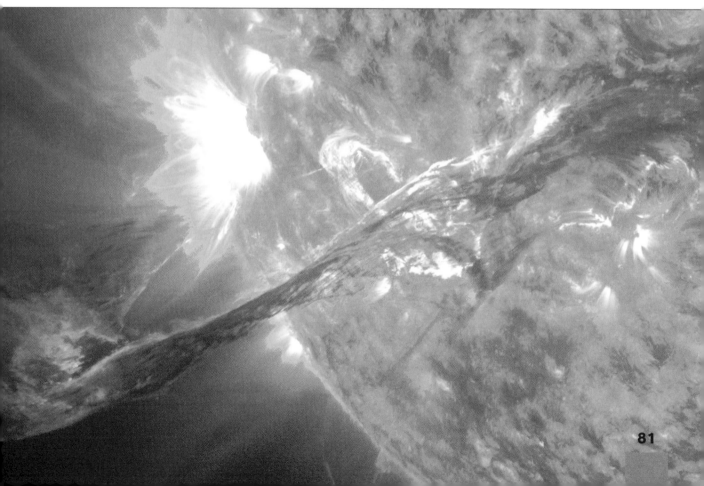

FAIRGROUND PHYSICS

WORDS TO KNOW

melting point: the temperature at which a solid turns into a liquid.

boiling point: the temperature at which a liquid turns into a gas.

condense: the process by which a gas cools and becomes a liquid.

sublimation: the process of a solid becoming a gas without going through the liquid phase.

deposition: the process in which a gas directly becomes a solid, without becoming a liquid first.

GOING THROUGH A PHASE!

When you add or remove energy—such as heat—from matter, you can make it change phases.

Adding heat to a solid, for instance, can turn it into a liquid. The added energy makes the molecules vibrate faster and move farther apart. When the substance reaches its **melting point**, it will start turning into a liquid. This is what happens to the ice cubes in your drink!

Every substance has its own melting point. Water's melting point is 32 degrees Fahrenheit (0 degrees Celsius), while a harder substance such as silver melts at 1,760 degrees Fahrenheit (960 degrees Celsius).

What happens if you add heat to a liquid? The molecules will again vibrate faster and move farther apart—until the liquid reaches its boiling point. Then, it starts turning into a gas. The **boiling point** of water, for example, is 212 degrees Fahrenheit (100 degrees Celsius).

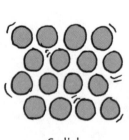

Solid

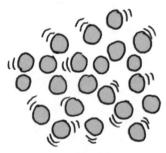

Liquid

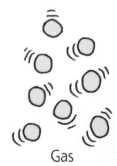

Gas

So far, we've added energy. What if we take away energy by cooling the substance? As the energy leaves the substance, its molecules slow down and move closer together. If you cool steam, it will **condense** back into liquid water. If you take even more heat away, the water will freeze into a solid.

If enough energy is applied, matter can even skip a state. For instance, ice can become water vapor. This is called **sublimation**. Some substances, such as dry ice, sublime naturally. That is, they go from solid to gas without becoming liquid first. Gases can also skip the liquid state and become solid. This process is called **deposition.**

How do we apply this to treats at the amusement park? First, we're going to take away some energy in order to make ice cream! Then, we're going to talk about using heat to fry foods. But first, the ice cream.

WE ALL SCREAM FOR . . .

Ice cream is basically milk (or cream), sugar, and flavoring cooled down to a solid state. But it's more than just a block of frozen milk. Ice cream is smooth and creamy, yet still solid. It's the size of the ice crystals that gives the ice cream its texture. If you have an ice cream maker, it churns and whips the mixture while lowering its temperature. This breaks up the ice crystals into tinier pieces.

Making ice cream!
credit: ilovebutter (CC BY 2.0)

WORDS TO KNOW

Middle Ages: the period of European history from about the years 350 to 1400.

dehydrate: to remove the moisture from something.

Maillard reaction: the chemical reaction between sugar and protein that gives browned foods their flavor.

Want to see how ice cream is made? **Check it out, from cow to ice cream shop!**

🔍 Kids should see ice cream

PS

Many myths surround the history of ice cream. Some say Italian explorer Marco Polo (1254–1324) brought it back with him from China. Others say Catherine de Medici (1519–1589) brought it to France from Italy when she married King Henry II.

Actually, ice cream is probably far older. Ancient Greeks and Romans enjoyed icy drinks. They harvested ice from the mountains and stored it in cool pits covered with straw. Chinese emperors of the Tang Dynasty (618–907) are thought to have been the first to enjoy a frozen, milk-like treat. This ice cream was made from heated milk thickened with flour and flavored with camphor, a substance harvested from evergreen trees. The mixture was poured in metal tubes and lowered into a pool of ice.

Other cultures made frozen desserts. In the **Middle Ages**, Arabs made chilled drinks flavored with fruit. They called these sharabt—or sherbet. By the seventeenth century, Europeans were making frozen desserts such as sorbets and gelatos.

Ice cream probably came to America in recipes carried by European settlers. The first ice cream parlor opened in New York in 1790. Founding father George Washington loved ice cream, as did Thomas Jefferson. And the sweet treat has skyrocketed in popularity as centuries have passed! Now, it's a favorite treat at the fairground.

The first official account of ICE CREAM in the United States dates to 1744. However, it wasn't until the late nineteenth century that ice cream became readily available to everyone.

COOKING WITH HEAT

Most of the treats at the amusement park are fried or baked. Let's look at how frying works. Cooking with fat or oil is called frying. The science is the same no matter how much oil you have in the

The MAILLARD REACTION is the chemical roller coaster that makes food golden brown and creates wonderful flavors.

pan. When the food hits the hot oil, its surface **dehydrates**. That is, the heat boils away the water from the food's surface, drying it out. Then, the sugars and proteins in the food start to break down to create both flavors and a golden brown surface. This is called the **Maillard reaction**.

You know who liked ice cream? Founding father Thomas Jefferson! **Check out his ice cream recipe at this website.** How does it compare to the stuff in your freezer?

🔎 Monticello ice cream

PS

Dulce de leche are milky treats formed through the Maillard reaction.
credit: Nicola (CC BY 2.0)

WORDS TO KNOW

amino acid: an organic compound that is used in every cell of the body to build proteins needed for survival.

compound: a substance made up of two or more elements.

organic: of living things.

conduction: the movement of heat or electricity through something, such as metal or water.

convection: movement in a gas or liquid in which the warmer parts rise up and the colder parts sink down.

Funneling Down the Gullet

Golden brown funnel cakes covered with powdered sugar are a favorite at fairs, carnivals, and amusement parks. Funnel cakes are made by pouring batter through a funnel onto a griddle. The first funnel cake may go back as far as the fourteenth century! A medieval cookbook from 1390 lists a basic recipe for a fried cake tossed with sugar and salt. The batter was poured through a hole in a bowl. Today, we associate funnel cakes with the Pennsylvania Dutch. They were German-speaking settlers who came to Pennsylvania in the seventeenth and eighteenth centuries. However, funnel cakes may not really be food from their culture. No one is quite sure. In 1952, a folk festival to promote Pennsylvania Dutch culture served funnel cakes—and they were a smash hit. Funnel cakes became a part of every Pennsylvania Dutch festival after that. Eventually, the treat made its way to other festivals, fairs, carnivals, and amusement parks.

In 1912, a French chemist named Louis Maillard (1878–1936) discovered how sugars and **amino acids** come together to create **compounds** that pack a lot of flavor. Amino acids are the **organic** building blocks of proteins, which are found in meats and other foods. Since Maillard's time, scientists have discovered that the Maillard reaction can create thousands of flavors, depending on the ingredients, cooking time, and temperature.

Most deep-fried food, such as those Oreos and pickles, are dipped in a batter. These give the treat a crispy crust. Why? When you plunge the food in the hot oil, all of its water bubbles to the surface. The batter forms a barrier between the rising water and the hot oil. The food inside steams while the batter cooks and crisps. After being removed from the oil, the food under the batter will continue to steam, keeping the outside crisp. When it cools, though, the water gets trapped—and you have soggy fried pickles! A starchy food such as a potato doesn't need a batter. Think French fries!

When there's a temperature difference, heat will flow from the higher to the lower temperature. In solids, we call this **conduction**. Remember, warming a solid causes molecules to vibrate more, making the heat spread.

Convection happens when you transfer heat by moving or displacing groups of molecules with higher-energy ones. This happens in liquids and gases. For example, when molecules of air heat up, they move around rapidly and start pushing the cooler, slower molecules out of the way. Warm air rises while cool air sinks. The same thing happens in a liquid. Warm water rises and cool water sinks. This is why boiling water and, later, steam rises in the funnel cake batter!

INSULATORS have **small air spaces** because air is not a good **CONDUCTOR**, so it makes it hard for the heat to vibrate the molecules. Styrofoam is a good insulator, which **is why it's often used for coolers and coffee cups.**

WORDS TO KNOW

ultraviolet (UV): a type of light with shorter wavelengths than visible light. Also called black light.

current: the steady flow of water or air in one direction.

SOLAR HEAT

Food isn't the only thing being cooked at the amusement park on a hot summer's day. You are, too! And so are the rides and the pavement. As you wait in line in the broiling, sticky heat, you might feel as though the sun is pouring all of its energy down on you.

More than 92 million miles away, the sun radiates energy in all directions. Most of it disappears into space. A sliver of the sun's energy hits the earth, enough to heat our planet and drive its weather. Only about half of the incoming solar energy makes it through to us. Some of the solar energy that hits the earth bounces off our atmosphere and back into space.

Solar panels convert the sun's rays into electrical energy.

Solar radiation is made up of heat, visible light, and **ultraviolet (UV)** rays. Matter—including the air, water, rocks, buildings, and living things—absorbs this energy. This heats the earth.

The planet doesn't heat evenly, though. Some areas get more solar energy than others. These differences drive the winds and ocean **currents**. Remember, heat flows from higher to lower temperatures!

Cooking With Light

Solar cookers let ultraviolet light in and convert it to heat. The cooker then traps the heat to cook the food. So, a cooker or oven needs three things: a reflective surface, a dark surface, and a clear/transparent lid or insulation. First, the reflective surface catches the sunlight and funnels it onto the dark surface, which absorbs the heat. Then, the clear cover insulator—such as a piece of glass or plastic—keeps heat from escaping. The insulator needs to be clear enough to let in sunlight. **You can explore more solar cookers at Solar Cookers International.**

solarcookers.org

WORDS TO KNOW

greenhouse gas: a gas in the atmosphere that traps heat. We need some greenhouse gases, but too many trap too much heat.

climate change: a change in long-term weather patterns, which can happen through natural or manmade processes.

climate crisis: the serious global problems related to climate change that are a result of human activity.

The average **TEMPERATURE** across the globe has risen about **1.62 degrees** Fahrenheit (0.9 degrees Celsius) since the late nineteenth century, mostly because of the increase in carbon dioxide and other **GREENHOUSE GASES** in the atmosphere emitted through human activities.

What would happen if the entire earth was heated constantly by the sun? It would grow hotter and hotter—and eventually not be able to support life. The earth actually radiates heat back out into space. However, the heat that gets in can get trapped in the atmosphere if it gets blocked by too much carbon dioxide or other **greenhouse gases.** When this happens, the earth begins heating up much as a greenhouse does, which is why this is called the greenhouse effect.

Can you imagine a day at the fair without some delicious treats? Heat and temperature play critical roles in amusement park fun. And when it gets too hot, it's time to take a dip in the wave pool. Even there, you're going to find some energy! We'll look at waves in the next chapter.

ESSENTIAL QUESTION

What's the difference between heat and temperature?

Climate Crisis

In recent decades, the greenhouse effect has caused major **climate change** and altered much of the earth's natural processes, including those that support life. People around the world are responding to the **climate crisis** by looking for ways to maintain a healthier balance of greenhouse gases in the atmosphere to prevent the earth's temperature from rising any higher. We are also working to reduce the amount of plastic debris in the oceans and on land to make healthier environments for all living things. Without these steps, the world will change drastically in the coming years.

ICE CREAM
IN A BAG

You can make ice cream without a fancy ice cream maker or even a freezer. You just need plastic baggies, ice, and salt. You'll be lowering the freezing point of the ice to make it even colder.

PHYSICS KIT

- ¼ cup sugar
- ½ cup milk
- ½ cup whipping cream
- ¼ teaspoon vanilla extract
- 1 quart sealable plastic bag
- 2 cups of ice
- 1 gallon sealable plastic bag
- thermometer
- ½ to ¾ cup table salt or rock salt

❯ Add the sugar, milk, cream, and vanilla to the smaller bag. Seal.

❯ Put the ice in the larger bag.

❯ Record the temperature of the ice.

❯ Add the salt to the ice.

❯ Place the sealed bag with the ice cream mixture inside the gallon bag with the ice.

❯ Seal the gallon bag.

❯ Gently rock or shake the larger bag for 10 to 15 minutes until the mixture in the smaller bag turns to ice cream. Tip: You might need to hold the bag with a dish towel. The ice will be colder than you expect!

❯ Open the gallon bag and record the temperature of the ice. Is it lower than you expected? Why?

❯ Take out the quart bag, open up the ice cream, and enjoy!

❯ How does this work? Adding salt to the ice lowers the freezing point of the ice. Salt water freezes at a lower temperature than fresh water. This makes the ice colder, which helps to freeze the ice cream mixture.

Try This!

Make different flavors! Try adding chocolate chips, crushed cookies, and nuts. Or use another flavor of extract you might have in the kitchen.

SOLAR OVEN
S'MORES

Solar power converts the sun's energy into electricity. Many buildings have solar panels on their roofs to do this. Your house or school might be powered this way—at least partially. But did you know you can cook with solar power? A few companies make solar stoves and ovens. We're going to make our own solar oven to bake some s'mores!

❯ **Close the pizza box lid.** You need to make an "oven door" flap in the top of the box. Draw a rectangle on the top that's almost as big as the lid. Leave about an inch all around the rectangle. Cut along three of the lines, the front and two sides, but leave the back one uncut. Fold the flap along this line.

❯ **Glue aluminum foil to the inside of the flap.** This will reflect the sun's rays onto the food.

❯ **Open the box.** Glue black construction paper along the bottom where the pizza would normally sit. This will help absorb the heat.

❯ **Tape plastic wrap over the "oven door" opening.** Tape this to the underside of the opening. This helps the air heat up inside the oven.

Watch this video about solar cookers. Why are these cookers so important?

🔎 Nat Geo solar cookers

Work in Renewable Energy!

Renewable energy is a fast-growing industry and there are many jobs available for people who are interested in making a difference in how the world works. Do some research on the following jobs and find one that appeals to you!

- Wind turbine technician
- Solar installer
- Alternative fuel engineer
- Sustainable architect
- Environmental engineer
- Farmer

- Wind energy developer
- Biochemist
- Green construction manager
- Renewable energy consultant
- Solar installer

> Optional step: Decorate your solar oven!

> Now, you're ready to cook! Assemble the s'mores and place them inside the oven on the black construction paper.

> Close the lid of the pizza box. Open the flap and prop it up with a skewer or other stick.

Try This!

Experiment with other foods. Does the oven get warm enough to heat a cup of cocoa or bake a cookie, for instance?

> Position the solar oven in the sun so that the sun's rays hit the aluminum foil and bounce down on the food. You may need to play with the position and angle of the oven.

> Wait for the chocolate and marshmallows to melt! How does your treat come out?

WORDS TO KNOW

renewable energy: a form of energy that doesn't get used up, including the energy of the sun and the wind.

HEAT-SENSITIVE
SLIME

PHYSICS KIT

- ¼ cup white school glue
- 1 tablespoon water
- food coloring, about 5 drops, maybe more
- 3 teaspoons thermochromic pigment (from a craft store or online)
- ¼ cup liquid starch

Ever see those coffee mugs that change colors or designs when you put a hot liquid in them? The design on the cup probably uses a **thermochromic** pigment. **Thermochromic materials change color when there's a change in temperature. Mood rings use them, too. We are going to make something more fun than a ring or coffee cup: slime that changes color with heat!**

❯ **First, decide on your color scheme.** The pigment will disappear when hot. The slime will be the color of the pigment and food coloring together when it's cold and the color of just the food coloring when warm. For instance, if you use blue pigment and yellow food coloring, the slime will be green when cool (blue + yellow) and then turn yellow when hot.

❯ **Mix the glue, water, food coloring, and pigment in a bowl.** The pigment should be evenly mixed throughout the glue.

❯ **Add about half of the liquid starch** and mix until thick and kind of slimy.

❯ **Knead the slime with your hands** to make sure all the glue is thoroughly mixed with the starch.

❯ **Add the rest of the starch and mix well.** Knead the slime until it's not sticky.

❯ **Now, you're ready to experiment with it!** Spread it out and place your hand on it. Does your hand change the color of the slime? Try placing the slime on something cold. What happens? Try putting it on something warm. Notice how the colors change.

Try This!

Make another batch using different colors!

WORDS TO KNOW

thermochromic: something that changes color when the temperature changes.

Chapter 6

RIDE THE
WAVES

It's a hot day at the park and you finally make it to the top of a giant water slide. You lie down on your back in the water, cross your arms, and gravity pulls you down the slide in a few seconds. You splash into the water at the bottom, creating waves that ripple across the pool. Fun!

Amusement parks, fairs, carnivals, and water parks all use a number of different waves, from the type you make when you splash in a pool to the type of waves that make up light and sounds in the park. As the sun goes down and the park lights up in neon brightness, it's waves that make that possible. The sing-song music coming from rides and game stalls? Made from waves! Let's look closer at this amazing **phenomenon**.

ESSENTIAL QUESTION

What is a wave and what is the role of a wave at the fairground?

WORDS TO KNOW

phenomenon: something seen or observed.

95

WORDS TO KNOW

medium: a substance, such as air or water, through which energy moves.

transverse wave: a wave that moves perpendicular to the direction in which the wave is moving.

crest: a tuft or ridge on top of a head or hill or wave.

trough: the lowest point between two hills or crests.

longitudinal wave: a wave that moves in the direction parallel to the direction that the wave is traveling.

surface wave: a wave that travels along or parallel to the earth's surface.

interface: a point where two systems, such as a wave and the shore, meet and interact.

frequency: the number of times something is repeated in a period of time.

amplitude: a measure of the movement of a wave.

wavelength: the length between two crests of a wave.

period: the length of time it takes for a wave to repeat itself.

Hertz (Hz): a unit of frequency, equal to one cycle per second.

WHAT IS A WAVE?

A wave is actually energy traveling through a **medium** such as water or air. Your body hitting the pool causes a disturbance, which makes the molecules of the water vibrate with energy. Each moving molecule sets the next one in motion and on and on. Those vibrations traveling through the medium—water in this case—translate into waves.

Did you know that the water isn't actually moving when you drop a pebble in the still water? It's the energy rippling outward, not the water molecules. Think of wind blowing through a wheat field. The stalks of wheat don't move down the field as the wind gusts by—they stay rooted in the ground. It's the energy that's moving down the field, not the wheat.

When you went down the slide into the pool, you released KINETIC ENERGY into the water in the pool, and the water responded with WAVES!

We typically think of waves looking like ones in the ocean. Actually, there are several types of waves. In each, the energy and particles move differently. The ocean wave is called a **transverse wave**. It **crests** and **troughs** like the surf, its particles moving up and down. A **longitudinal wave** spirals in a straight line like the coils in a spring—or slinky. In this kind of wave, the particles move back and forth. In a **surface wave**, the energy ripples and the particles travel in circles. These waves happen where the water meets an **interface** or boundary. Think ripples in a coffee cup or in shallow water.

TRANSVERSE WAVES

For most of this chapter, we'll talk about transverse waves because they're easiest to visualize, but other types of waves have similar properties, such as **frequency** and **amplitude**.

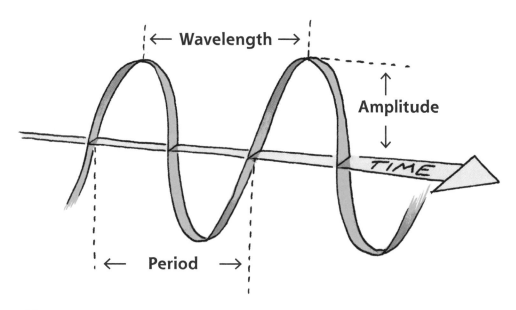

Transverse waves rise and fall equally around an imaginary middle line. Think of this as the wave's resting position. In the ocean, this is the sea level. The top of the wave is called the crest, while the bottom is the trough. The **wavelength** is the distance from crest to crest. The amplitude is the distance above the resting position. The wave repeats itself going from crest to trough to crest. The time it takes to do this is called a **period**. You can also measure the period by timing how long a complete wavelength takes to pass one location.

When describing waves, another important term is frequency. This is the number of times a wave cycles past a certain point in a second. In other words, frequency is the speed at which the wave is traveling. Frequencies are usually measured in **Hertz (Hz)** or megahertz (mHz). Those might sound familiar! More on this later.

WORDS TO KNOW

vibrate: to move back and forth or side to side very quickly.

amplify: to make a sound louder.

pitch: how high or low a sound is, depending on its frequency.

SOUND WAVES

What would a carnival, fair, or amusement park be like without sound? Think of the music playing on the rides, the screams from the roller coaster, and even the sounds of the bumper cars smashing into each other.

Sounds are made by a **vibrating** source, such as speaker or crashing car. The resulting waves travel through a medium and then hit our ears. A sound must have a medium to pass through. The medium can be solid, gas, or liquid. Usually, we think of sounds as passing through air, but you can hear underwater. The sounds might be a bit muffled or not as clear as through the air. You can also hear through some solids, too, such as steel or concrete.

The speed of sound isn't constant. Sounds pass through different materials at different speeds. Even temperature can affect the speed of sound. For example, the speed of sound through air is 343 miles per second at 20 degrees Celsius and 355 miles per second at 40 degrees Celsius.

How We Hear

Sound waves enter our outer ear and travel down the ear canal to the eardrum. The eardrum vibrates, sending vibrations to the three little bones in your middle ear: the incus, malleus, and stapes. These bones **amplify** the sound and send them to the

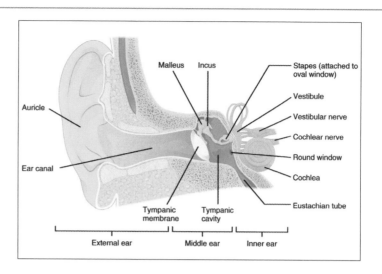

credit: OpenStax (CC BY 2.0)

inner ear, or cochlea. The vibrations activate tiny hair cells in the inner ear, which in turn activate the auditory nerve to carry the information to the brain. Your brain translates this information into sound you understand.

At 20 degrees Celsius, the speed of sound is 1,481 miles per second in water and 4,600 miles per second through copper. You can actually hear better through a solid such as copper than through the air!

The amusement park is full of many kinds of sounds. Some are music, some are pure tones, and some are noise. Musical sounds have regular vibrations. Your ear picks out the frequencies of sound, which we think of as **pitch**. (Remember, frequency is how fast the wavelength of a particular sound is traveling.) Non-musical sounds are more complex. They might be a mix of differing and even changing frequencies. Different sources emit different frequencies. For instance, voices fall in the range of 200 Hz to 8,000 Hz. A car horn might blare at 350 Hz, while a pesky mosquito hums away at around 18,000 Hz.

SOUNDS travel through most MEDIUMS, including air, water, and solids, as a LONGITUDINAL WAVE. Sound can also travel as a TRANSVERSE WAVE through solids.

FAIRGROUND PHYSICS

As you walk through the amusement park, many sounds are probably hitting your ears. But did you know that you can't actually hear all of them? You might not hear a really low vibration from a nearby earthquake. And you might not hear a really high vibration from a bat. Humans can normally only hear vibrations with a frequency between 20 and 20,000 Hz. Anything above that range we call **ultrasound**, and anything below that range is **infrasound**.

Different species have vastly different HEARING RANGES. Blue whales can hear between 14 and 36 Hz, while bats can hear between 2,000 and 120,000 Hz.

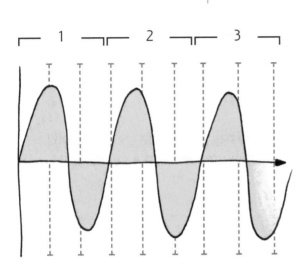

Wave A
(higher frequency)

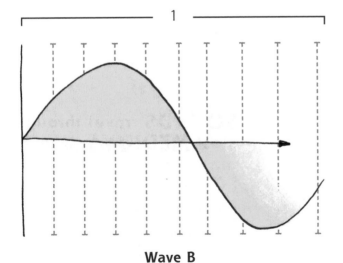

Wave B
(lower frequency)

Infrasound—sound below 20 Hz—can be produced by natural events, such as earthquakes, severe storms, volcanoes, avalanches, and waterfalls. We can produce infrasound with heavy machinery, explosions, and even specialized sound speakers. Many animals, including whales and elephants, use low-frequency sound to communicate across great distances.

Doppler Effect

Ever notice how the screams on the roller coaster or the music on the carousel changes in pitch as the sound moves away or toward you? The same thing happens with an ambulance, its siren blaring. As it comes toward you, the pitch of the siren gets higher. The pitch gets lower as it moves away from you. When a source of sound is stationary, or not moving, equally spaced waves move away from its center. However, if the source is moving, the sound waves get squashed coming toward you or stretched out as they move away from you. This is called the **Doppler effect**.

Other animals use ultrasound—sound above 20,000 Hz—to communicate and guide them. For instance, bats send out ultrasonic pings between 50,000 and 10,000 Hz in order to navigate around structures. Dolphins and some whales use ultrasound to navigate, too.

Humans use ULTRASOUND for many purposes. Doctors use ultrasonic imaging to examine babies before they are born. Ultrasound can also be used to examine machinery for defects and for cleaning.

Take a listen to different marine animals at this website. Some of these had to be altered simply so humans could hear them. Why do you think they all sound so different? What might we sound like to them?

🔎 Discovery sound sea

Can you hear some of the deep infrasound from forest elephants? Test how low you can go!

🔎 Elephant Listening Project

WORDS TO KNOW

electromagnetic (EM) spectrum: the entire range of radiation that includes high-energy cosmic rays and gamma rays, X-rays, radio waves, short microwaves, ultraviolet and infrared light, and visible light.

ELECTROMAGNETIC WAVES are TRANSVERSE WAVES. They also have both an **ELECTRIC** and a **MAGNETIC** wave field. These fields are at right angles to the direction the wave travels.

LIGHT WAVES

Fairs and amusement parks also use another type of wave—light! All the rides are usually covered in lights, many of them neon. We might also watch brilliant fireworks at the end of the evening or on a special occasion.

Light is an electromagnetic wave. It carries energy as both electricity and magnetism. Light is given off—or radiates—from matter, such as a light bulb or the sun. All electromagnetic waves travel at the same speed—the speed of light—through a vacuum. Electromagnetic waves have different frequencies and wavelengths, forming what we call the **electromagnetic (EM) spectrum**.

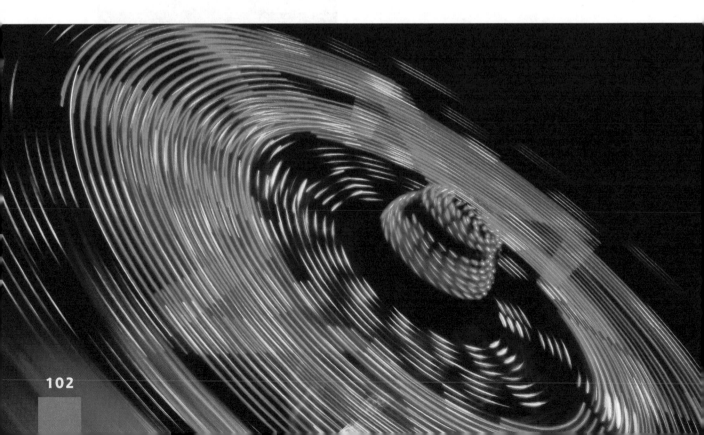

How Do We See?

Light rays from an object enter the eye. The cornea, the lens, and the jelly-like fluid in the eye focus the light on the retina at the back of the eye. This produces an inverted image. The light-sensitive cells create nerve impulses. The optic nerve sends this information to the brain. How do we see color? Special cells on the retina called rods and cones are sensitive to different frequencies—or colors—of light!

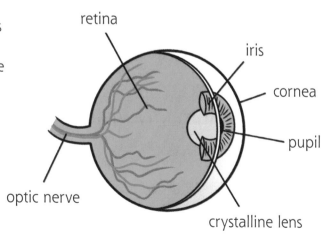

WORDS TO KNOW

visible light: light you can see.

gamma ray: light that has the shortest wavelength and highest energy.

infrared (IR): a type of light with a longer wavelength than visible light, which can also be felt as heat.

noble gas: a group of seven chemical elements that are naturally occurring and very stable.

photon: a particle of light.

There has been some debate through the centuries whether light really is a WAVE or a PARTICLE—or both. Some experiments proved it to be one— others have proven it to be both.

Humans can see only a small sliver of the EM spectrum. This is called **visible light**, and it's divided into the colors of the rainbow: red, orange, yellow, green, blue, indigo, and violet. Red light has the lower frequency and violet has the highest.

Above violet are ultraviolet light, X-rays, and **gamma rays**. Coming from the sun, UV light is responsible for suntans— and sunburns. X-rays and gamma rays are forms of radiation. You've probably had an X-ray at the doctor's or dentist's office.

Below the visible spectrum are **infrared (IR)** light, microwaves, and radio waves. IR light includes heat. Everything emits IR radiation in the form of heat. This can be detected by the sensors used in night vision goggles and IR cameras. Microwaves are often used for communications, radar, and cooking! And radio waves are used for communication—and to carry sounds and music.

The EM spectrum arranges electromagnetic waves in order of decreasing wavelength and increasing energy and frequency. Humans can see light only in the visible part of the spectrum.
credit: Johannes Ahlmann (CC BY 2.0)

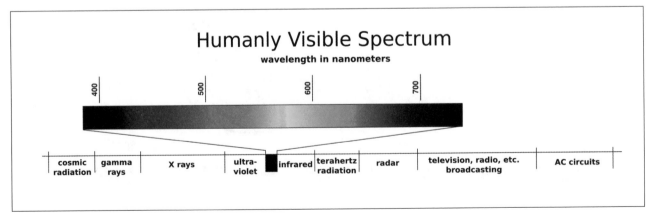

NEON LIGHTS

Many amusement parks use neon lights in their signs. In 1910, French chemist George Claude (1870–1960) was the first person to apply electricity to a tube of neon, creating a neon lamp. In the 1920s, his company started selling neon signs in America. These signs became immediately popular for outdoor advertising.

How do they work? A neon light has a glass tube containing a small amount of neon gas, a **noble gas** that was discovered in 1898. When electricity is passed through the tube, the neon atoms release a light particle called a **photon**. Each noble gas emits a certain color photon. Neon photons are red-orange. To get other colors, light makers use other noble gases or a mixture of them. Helium emits a pink light. Argon is blue. Krypton is green.

The word NEON comes from the Greek word *neos*, which means "new gas."

WORDS TO KNOW

concave: a surface that curves inward like the inside of a bowl.

convex: a surface that curves outward like the outside of a bowl.

As you can see, the fairground is not only a good place to have a good time, it's also an excellent place to learn some science! From roller coasters and drop towers to funnel cakes and ice cream, from the music to the neon lights, your time at the fair is governed by the laws of physics. So, strap in and have fun!

ESSENTIAL QUESTION

What is a wave and what is the role of a wave at the fairground?

Fun House Mirrors and Reflections

Many amusement parks and carnivals have a hall of mirrors. How do reflections work? Waves! When a wave strikes a surface, the energy can be absorbed, reflected, refracted, or all of the above. Light waves will bounce off a smooth or shiny surface, such as a mirror. We call this reflection. The reflected light ray will bounce off the surface of the mirror at the same angle as the incoming ray hit it. This is called the law of reflection. Fun houses use mirrors that distort your image to make you look really skinny or very short. To do this, the carnival uses mirrors that are curved.

There are generally two types of curved mirrors: **concave** and **convex**. In a concave mirror, the center part is curved inward. This makes you look thin and tall. A convex mirror bulges outward in the center, making you look short and fat!

credit: Nan Palmero (CC BY 2.0)

NOISEMAKER
DOPPLER EFFECT

PHYSICS KIT
° index card
° popsicle stick
° craft foam
° rubber band

Amusement parks are full of sounds. They're often moving either away from you or toward you. The sounds change pitch as they do. This is called the Doppler effect. Make a simple noisemaker to experiment with this phenomenon.

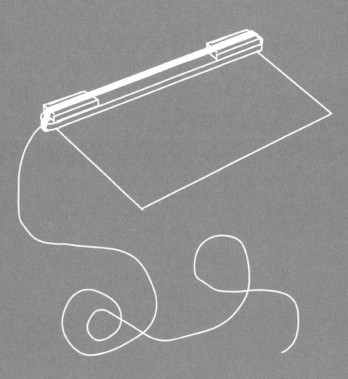

❱ Center and tape a 3-by-5-inch index card to a popsicle stick, lengthwise. The long edge of the index card should be lined up with the long edge of the popsicle stick.

❱ Cut out two small strips of craft foam. They should be the same width as the popsicle stick. Tape the craft foam over the ends of the popsicle stick. In other words, cap the ends with craft foam!

❱ Stretch a rubber band lengthwise across the caps of the popsicle stick.

❱ Tie a string around one end of the noisemaker. Be careful not to tie down the rubber band.

❱ Now, you're ready to make some noise! Hold onto the string and swirl the noisemaker around your head. Listen carefully. Does the noise it make sound higher or lower as it moves toward you?

Try This!

Use a longer string (or a shorter one!) to swing your noisemaker. Does this make a difference in the sound? Does it make the Doppler effect easier to hear? Do you have to expend more energy to make the noisemaker go?

MINI
DUNK TANK

PHYSICS KIT
- ° cardboard
- ° 2- to 3-foot lightweight dowel
- ° shoebox
- ° weight or brick
- ° bowl
- ° small shelf brackets
- ° screws or hot glue
- ° small toy or mini figurine
- ° ping pong ball

Fairs and carnivals usually have many booths with games. One of the most popular is the dunk tank. You get to throw a ball at a target for a chance to drop a person into a tank of water. For this activity, make a mini version of a dunk tank and send a toy or mini figurine into a bowl of water!

CAUTION: Ask an adult to help with the glue gun.

❯ **First, make the dunker and target.** Draw a target on a piece of cardboard and cut it out. Glue or tape the target on one end of the lightweight dowel.

❯ **Cut out an equal-sized square piece of cardboard.** This is the counterweight for the other end of the stick. Decorate it, if you like!

❯ **Glue or tape the counterweight** to the other end of the dowel.

❯ **For the dunk tower,** stand a shoebox or other small- to medium-sized box on its end. Place something heavy, such as a weight or brick, inside so that the tower won't topple over.

❯ **Cut out a piece of heavy cardboard to create a ledge.** The ledge should be slightly smaller than the bowl you'll use in the next step. Attach this to the side of the dunk tower using small shelf brackets. You can use screws or hot glue.

❯ **Hot glue a small hinge to the top side of the ledge.** The hinge will flip a bowl off the ledge.

Carnival Game Scams!

The dunk tank is just one of many carnival games you can find at the fair or amusement park. You've probably played ring toss or skeeball. And you might have even won a prize. Some games, though, are really hard to win. They are often designed that way! For instance, the hoop at the basketball shooting booth might actually be higher than a regulation one. Or the rings in the ring toss game might just barely fit over the targets. This makes it nearly impossible to win.

Watch a former NASA engineer investigate some carnival games and explain the scientific reasons why they're scams.

🔎 carnival scam science

❯ Glue the bottom of a small plastic or paper bowl to the top side of the hinge. The bowl shouldn't sit too flatly on the ledge—otherwise, the dunking arm won't be able to flip it up.

❯ Place the dowel of the dunking arm between the bowl and the box with the target facing forward.

❯ Put a bowl of water under the dunking ledge, and load something small—a marble or mini figurine—in the bowl.

❯ Throw a ping pong ball at the target. When you hit the target, the dunking arm should flip the bowl over, sending its contents into the water. You may need to adjust the position of the dunking arm or the bowl on the ledge to get it to flip.

❯ Observe the wave patterns when the object hits the water.

Try This!

Put different-sized objects in the dunking bowl. Do you have to exert more force or throw harder to get the bowl to flip? Does the heavier object make bigger waves? Why do you think this happens?

DIY FUN HOUSE
MIRRORS

Carnivals, fun houses, and even haunted houses often have mirrors that distort how you look. They make you look really tall and thin—or short and wide. The trick is in the shape of the mirror. Some bulge outward, while some cave inward. We're going to make our own fun house mirror!

> **Measure the height and width of the frame.** Add an inch or so to the length.

> **Cut out the poster board** to fit the above measurements. You want the board a little longer than the frame.

> **Cut the Mylar** to the same size as the poster board.

> **Spray adhesive evenly** on the poster board.

> **Carefully apply the Mylar.** Smooth it out so that there are no bubbles. The surface should be shiny and smooth like a mirror. Let dry. This is your mirror!

> **Insert the mirror into the frame.** It will be too long, so you'll need to curve the surface of the mirror to make it fit.

> **Look at yourself in the fun house mirror!** Is your image distorted? Do you look thin or wide? Play around with the curve of the mirror to see how it changes your image.

Try This!

Create another mirror with a bigger bulge in the middle. How does that affect your image?

MAKE YOUR OWN
CHLADNI PLATE

PHYSICS KIT

- smartphone/tablet with a frequency sound generator app
- wireless speaker
- mixing bowl
- parchment paper and rubber band
- salt (optional: dye the salt with food coloring)

In the eighteenth century, German scientist Ernst Chladni (1756–1827) did several important experiments with sound. He spread salt or sand on thin metal plates and then made them vibrate using a cello bow. The salt moved in beautiful patterns, collecting in some spots and not in others. He figured out that the places where the salt didn't collect were being moved by sound waves. Today, you're going to create a twenty-first-century version!

You can watch a demonstration in this video.

🔎 Smithsonian Chladni plates

▶ **Turn on the wireless speaker** and place it in the mixing bowl.

▶ **Cover the bowl** with parchment paper and secure tightly with a rubber band. The paper should be very tight.

▶ **Pour salt on the parchment paper and spread it out.** This shouldn't be too thick. You can dye the salt with food coloring or use pink salt so that you can more easily see the salt move.

▶ **Download a free app** that will create sound at specific frequencies—with adult permission, of course! There are several of these for iOS and Android.

▶ **Play a tone at a lower frequency using the app.** What happens to the salt? Experiment with different frequencies. Are there some you can't hear? How does the parchment paper vibrate?

Try This!

Play some music or other sounds. How does the salt react? What patterns does it make?

PAPER
CIRCUITS

PHYSICS KIT
- ° paper
- ° graphite pencil (2B or harder)
- ° LED light
- ° 9-volt battery

The rides and lights at amusement parks and fairs run on electricity. In a neon light, for instance, electricity travels from a power source to the neon bulb over wires. The path the electricity follows is called a circuit. But you don't need wires to make a circuit. You can actually draw one on paper!

CAUTION: Have an adult help you with the battery.

❯ Draw a simple design—such as a circle or square—on a piece of paper with a graphite art pencil. You can get these at art or craft stores.

❯ Leave a small gap, about ¼ inch, in the line on both the right and left sides of the drawing. (You can erase the line to create the gaps.) The battery and light will go in these gaps. Make the graphite lines thick without any breaks in them (except the gaps mentioned) for the best results.

Copper Tape Circuits

You can also use copper tape to create circuits on paper. Copper is a better conductor of electricity. Copper tape is available in a variety of widths at most craft and hobby stores. You can also find it at home improvement and gardening stores, where it's often sold as slug and snail repellent!

➤ **Take the ends of the LED light** and separate them a bit. One end will be a bit longer than the other.

➤ **Tape the ends of the LED to the lines** on the right side of the page. The light part of the LED should be in the gap.

➤ **Place the 9-volt battery** upside down in the gap on the left side of the drawing. The battery's positive and negative terminals should each touch one of the lines. You may need to switch the battery around to get them to line up. The LED should light up.

WHAT'S HAPPENING?

This works because the graphite in the pencil is an electrical conductor—just like copper wire. A conductor is a material that electricity can travel through. Graphite isn't as good a conductor as copper, though.

Try This!

Play around with different designs. Does the length or width of the line make a difference in how bright the light is?

4-D coaster: a roller coaster where the seats are attached to the sides of the track, making riders spin and flip much more than on a regular roller coaster.

absolute zero: the point at which atoms in a substance stop moving and no more energy can be taken out.

acceleration: the rate at which the speed of a moving object changes through time.

accelerometer: a device that measures changes in speed and direction.

adrenaline: a hormone produced in high-stress situations. Also called epinephrine.

air resistance: the force of air pushing against an object.

amino acid: an organic compound that is used in every cell of the body to build proteins needed for survival.

amplify: to make a sound louder.

amplitude: a measure of the movement of a wave.

ancestor: an earlier form from which something modern has developed. Also a person from your family or culture who lived before you.

arc: a section of a curve or part of a circle.

atmosphere: the blanket of gases around the earth.

atom: the smallest particle of a substance that can exist by itself or be combined with other atoms to form a molecule.

BCE: put after a date, BCE stands for Before Common Era and counts years down to zero. CE stands for Common Era and counts years up from zero. This book was published in 2020 CE.

bladder: a sac of tissue in the body of animals that holds urine.

boardwalk: a walkway along a beach or waterfront, typically made of wood.

boiling point: the temperature at which a liquid turns into a gas.

catapult: a device used to hurl or launch something.

centrifugal force: the outward force on an object moving in a curved path around another object.

centrifuge: a machine with a rapidly rotating container that applies centrifugal force to its contents to separate fluids of different densities or liquids from solids.

centripetal force: a force that pulls an object moving in a circular path toward the center of its path.

chemical energy: energy from a chemical reaction.

circuit: the complete path traveled by an electric current.

climate change: a change in long-term weather patterns, which can happen through natural or manmade processes.

climate crisis: the serious global problems related to climate change that are a result of human activity.

compound: a substance made up of two or more elements.

compressed air: air under more pressure than the outside air.

concave: a surface that curves inward like the inside of a bowl.

concessions: an area for selling food and drinks at a fair or amusement park.

condense: the process by which a gas cools and becomes a liquid.

conduction: the movement of heat or electricity through something, such as metal or water.

conductive: describes a material or object that allows electricity or heat to move through it.

conductor: a material through which electricity and heat move easily.

conservation: in physics, when certain physical properties do not change in a physical system. For example, momentum isn't lost or created when two objects hit each other.

constant acceleration: the steady rate at which a falling object picks up speed.

convection: movement in a gas or liquid in which the warmer parts rise up and the colder parts sink down.

convex: a surface that curves outward like the outside of a bowl.

crest: a tuft or ridge on top of a head or hill or wave.

current: the steady flow of water or air in one direction.

dehydrate: to remove the moisture from something.

denser: more mass in the same space.

deposition: the process in which a gas directly becomes a solid, without becoming a liquid first.

diameter: a straight line running from one side of a circle to the other through the center.

dilute: to make thinner or weaker through the addition of distance or material.

Doppler effect: a change in the frequency of waves that occurs as an object changes position with respect to an observer.

electrical current: the flow of electrons through a material.

electrical energy: energy related to electricity.

electromagnetic: one of the fundamental forces of the universe, which is responsible for magnetic attraction and electrical charges.

electromagnetic (EM) spectrum: the entire range of radiation that includes high-energy cosmic rays and gamma rays, X-rays, radio waves, short microwaves, ultraviolet and infrared light, and visible light.

electromagnetism: magnetism created by a current of electricity.

electron: a negatively charged particle swirling around the nucleus of an atom.

element: a pure substance that cannot be broken down into a simpler substance. Everything in the universe is made up of combinations of elements. Oxygen and gold are two elements.

ellipse: an oval shape.

energy: the ability to do work or cause change.

engineer: someone who uses science, math, and creativity to design and build things.

exhibition: a public show of art or other interesting things.

fight-or-flight response: the brain's response to defend itself against or flee from a perceived threat.

force: a push or pull that changes an object's motion.

free fall: the motion of an object being acted upon only by the force of gravity, as if it were falling from the sky.

frequency: the number of times something is repeated in a period of time.

friction: the force that slows a moving object or objects when they move against each other.

fundamental: a central or primary rule or principle on which something is based.

gamma ray: light that has the shortest wavelength and highest energy.

gondola: a small passenger carriage used to carry people.

gravitational: relating to the force of gravity.

gravity: a force that pulls all objects toward the earth.

greenhouse gas: a gas in the atmosphere that traps heat. We need some greenhouse gases, but too many trap too much heat.

Hertz (Hz): a unit of frequency, equal to one cycle per second.

hexagon: a shape with six equal sides.

hormone: a chemical that carries signals from one part of the body to another.

hydraulic: describes a system that pushes and pulls objects using the motion of water or other liquids.

impulse: the force and time that transfers momentum from one object to another.

inertia: the tendency of an object to resist a change in motion. An object in motion tends to stay in motion and an object at rest tends to stay at rest.

infrared (IR): a type of light with a longer wavelength than visible light, which can also be felt as heat.

infrasound: sound that is lower in frequency than 20 Hz.

innovative: coming up with new ideas or methods of doing things.

insulator: a material that allows little or no heat, electricity, or sound to go into or out of something.

interact: how things that are together affect each other.

interface: a point where two systems, such as a wave and the shore, meet and interact.

inversely: when something increases in relation to a decrease in another thing or vice versa.

inverse square law: the principle in physics that the effect of certain forces on an object varies by the inverse square of the distance between the object and the source of the force.

invert: to turn upside down.

kinetic energy: energy caused by movement.

landscaping: an area of land with special features, such as pools and gardens.

launch system: a system that propels a roller coaster into motion.

longitudinal wave: a wave that moves in the direction parallel to the direction that the wave is traveling.

Maillard reaction: the chemical reaction between sugar and protein that gives browned foods their flavor.

mass: the amount of material that an object contains.

matter: what an object is made of. Anything that has weight and takes up space.

mechanical energy: energy related to motion and height.

medium: a substance, such as air or water, through which energy moves.

melting point: the temperature at which a solid turns into a liquid.

microgravity: when something acts as though there is no gravity because it is in free fall or in orbit around the earth.

Middle Ages: the period of European history from about the years 350 to 1400.

midway: an area of sideshows, games of chance or skill, and other amusements at a fair or exhibition.

molecular: having to do with molecules, the groups of atoms bound together to form everything.

molecule: the simplest part of an element (such as oxygen) or a compound (such as water). Molecules are made up of combinations of atoms, which are the smallest particles of matter.

momentum: a force that keeps an object moving after it has begun to move.

monorail: a railroad in which the track consists of a single raised rail, with the trains suspended from it or balancing on it.

navigate: to find your way from one place to another.

neutron: a particle in the nucleus of an atom that does not have a charge.

Newtonian physics: the science that uses the laws of motion and gravitation formulated in the late seventeenth century by English physicist Sir Isaac Newton to explain how matter behaves.

noble gas: a group of seven chemical elements that are naturally occurring and very stable.

nonconductor: a material that does not conduct electricity.

nuclear energy: energy produced by a nuclear reaction, typically the splitting of an atom.

nucleus: the central part of an atom. Plural is nuclei.

orbit: the path of an object circling another object in space.

organic: of living things.

particle: a tiny piece of matter.

patent: a document from the government that gives an inventor the exclusive right to make, use, or sell his or her invention.

pendulum: a weight hung from a fixed point that swings back and forth due to gravity.

period: the length of time it takes for a wave to repeat itself.

perpendicular: a line at an angle of 90 degrees to another line or surface. The two lines form a corner, called a right angle.

phenomenon: something seen or observed.

photon: a particle of light.

physicist: a scientist who studies physics.

physics: the study of physical forces, including matter, energy, and motion, and how these forces interact with each other.

pitch: how high or low a sound is, depending on its frequency.

plasma: one of the states of matter. The sun, stars, and lightning are made of plasma.

pleasure garden: a garden open to the public that offers entertainment.

pleasure wheel: an early ancestor of the Ferris wheel.

plummet: to fall quickly.

pneumatic: describes a system that pushes and pulls objects using tubes filled with air or other gases.

potential energy: energy that is stored.

proportional: corresponding in size or amount to something else.

proton: a particle in the nucleus of an atom that has a positive charge.

psychological: relating to or affecting the mind.

quanta: in quantum physics, a specific amount of energy. Plural is quantum.

quantum physics: an area of physics founded on the idea that light energy is made of different packets of energy.

radiant energy: energy from light.

radiation: energy that comes from a source and travels through something, such as the radiation from an X-ray that travels through a person.

radius: a straight line from the center of a circle or sphere to any point on the outer edge.

renewable energy: a form of energy that doesn't get used up, including the energy of the sun and the wind.

repel: to push away or apart.

resort: a place that is a popular destination for vacations.

Russian Mountain: a wooden hill structure covered in ice that riders slid down in wooden sleds.

satellite: a manmade object placed in orbit in space used to gather information or to make communication possible.

Scientific Revolution: a series of events and discoveries between the 1500s and 1700s that marked the emergence of modern science.

semiconductor: a material such as silicon that can vary the amount of electrical charge it will carry depending on certain conditions.

souvenir: something that you keep to remind you of a special place you visited.

space time: the concept that time and three-dimensional space act on each other and exist together in a four-dimensional continuum. Also called the space-time continuum.

spectrum: a band of colors that a ray of light can be separated into to measure properties of the object, including motion and composition. Plural is spectra.

speed: the distance an object travels in a unit of time.

staple: something used regularly.

static electricity: electricity that collects on the surface of something and does not flow as a current. It can cause a mild shock if you touch it.

strong force: a fundamental force that works inside the nucleus of an atom.

subatomic: relating to the inside of an atom.

sublimation: the process of a solid becoming a gas without going through the liquid phase.

surface wave: a wave that travels along or parallel to the earth's surface.

technology: the tools, methods, and systems used to solve a problem or do work.

theory: an unproven idea that explains why something is the way it is.

thermochromic: something that changes color when the temperature changes.

transverse wave: a wave that moves perpendicular to the direction in which the wave is moving.

trolley: a small train powered by electricity from an overhead cable. Also called a cable car.

trough: the lowest point between two hills or crests.

ultrasound: sound that is higher in frequency than 20,000 Hz.

ultraviolet (UV): a type of light with shorter wavelengths than visible light. Also called black light.

universe: everything that exists, everywhere.

vacuum: a space with nothing in it, not even air.

velocity: a measure of an object's speed and direction.

vibrate: to move back and forth or side to side very quickly.

visible light: light you can see.

wavelength: the length between two crests of a wave.

weak force: a fundamental force that works inside the nucleus of an atom.

work: the force applied to an object to move it across a distance.

world fair: an international exhibition of technology, science, and culture.

Metric Conversions

Use this chart to find the metric equivalents to the English measurements in this book. If you need to know a half measurement, divide by two. If you need to know twice the measurement, multiply by two. How do you find a quarter measurement? How do you find three times the measurement?

English	Metric
1 inch	2.5 centimeters
1 foot	30.5 centimeters
1 yard	0.9 meter
1 mile	1.6 kilometers
1 pound	0.5 kilogram
1 teaspoon	5 milliliters
1 tablespoon	15 milliliters
1 cup	237 milliliters

BOOKS

Colón, Erica I., Ph.D. *Awesome Physics Experiments for Kids: 40 Fun Science Projects and Why They Work.* Rockridge Press, 2019.

Macaulay, David. *The Way Things Work Now.* HMH Books for Young Readers, 2016.

Schul, Christina. *Awesome Engineering Activities for Kids: 50+ Exciting STEAM Projects to Design and Build.* Rockridge Press, 2019.

WEBSITES

Amusement Park Physics (PBS/Annenberg Learner): learner.org/interactives/parkphysics

Crash Course Physics (PBS Digital Studios/Crash Course): youtube.com/channel/UCX6b17PVsYBQ0ip5gyeme-Q

Crash Course Kids (Engineering and Physical Science): youtube.com/user/crashcoursekids

PBS Learning Media: pbslearningmedia.org/subjects/science/physical-science

ESSENTIAL QUESTIONS

Introduction: What makes fairgrounds fun?

Chapter 1: Do people love carnival rides today for the same reasons they loved them in the last century?

Chapter 2: How do bumper cars move? Why do they bounce?

Chapter 3: What makes objects move? What is force?

Chapter 4: How do roller coasters get their energy?

Chapter 5: What's the difference between heat and temperature?

Chapter 6: What is a wave and what is the role of a wave at the fairground?

QR CODE GLOSSARY

page 2: youtube.com/watch?v=ABQx3Sue10o

page 5: youtube.com/watch?time_continue=220&v=E43-CfukEgs

page 5: youtube.com/watch?time_continue=48&v=4mTsrRZEMwA

page 19: youtu.be/U84e4Oq8tqQ

page 22: youtube.com/watch?v=1z7R-_St_gw

page 25: youtube.com/watch?v=_qWmwtGZipw

page 28: learner.org/interactives/parkphysics/bumpercars

page 32: youtube.com/watch?v=36_fbLCWb-4

page 35: youtube.com/watch?v=OuA-znVMY3I

page 37: roadandtrack.com/car-culture/entertainment/videos/a33078/watch-the-stig-set-a-guinness-world-record-in-a-100-mph-bumper-car

page 38: youtube.com/watch?v=PcGIUZzWoVc

page 41: youtu.be/SRo4rjyczOk

page 44: youtube.com/watch?v=MTY1Kje0yLg

page 45: youtube.com/watch?v=xQ4znShlK5A

page 45: youtube.com/watch?v=KDp1tiUsZw8

page 47: youtube.com/watch?v=GFWsYJ0_KMI

page 49: youtube.com/watch?v=yVw8Fex5ZAQ

page 52: youtube.com/watch?v=2V9h42yspbo

page 59: youtube.com/watch?v=fAqa982j1a0

page 64: pbs.org/video/how-rollercoasters-are-made-bpyhdv

page 68: youtu.be/jWh9NfFdRE4

page 73: architecturelab.net/furl-soft-pneumatic-pavilion

page 84: thekidshouldseethis.com/post/how-is-ice-cream-made

page 85: monticello.org/site/research-and-collections/ice-cream

page 89: solarcookers.org

page 92: youtube.com/watch?v=Ofn7jqPDTeY

page 101: dosits.org/galleries/audio-gallery

page 101: elephantlisteningproject.org/all-about-infrasound

page 109: youtube.com/watch?v=tk_ZlWJ3qJl

page 111: youtube.com/watch?v=KEttRmu2kGk

INDEX